The
Nature-Friendly Garden

Creating a Backyard Haven
for Plants, Wildlife, and People

Marlene A. Condon

Copyright © 2006 by Stackpole Books

Published by
STACKPOLE BOOKS
5067 Ritter Rd.
Mechanicsburg, PA 17055
www.stackpolebooks.com

Printed in China

First edition

10 9 8 7 6 5 4 3 2 1

Cover design by Caroline Stover

All photographs by the author

Cover photographs: Top: Eight-spotted Forester moth (Alypia octomaculata) *on* Lantana camara; *Middle: Gray Treefrog* (Hyla versicolor); *Bottom: Red-phase Eastern Screech-Owl* (Megascops asio); *Background: Lamppost with Clematis*

Library of Congress Cataloging-in-Publication Data

Condon, Marlene A.
   The nature-friendly garden : creating a backyard haven for plants, wildlife, and people / Marlene A. Condon.
      p. cm.
   Includes bibliographical references and index.
   ISBN-13: 978-0-8117-3261-1 (alk. paper)
   ISBN-10: 0-8117-3261-4 (alk. paper)
   1. Landscape gardening. 2. Natural landscaping. 3. Gardening to attract wildlife. I. Title.
SB473.C652 2006
639.9'2—dc22

2005030354

This book is dedicated to:

Donna Bennett, who first encouraged me
to share my nature observations with the public;
Dave and Judy Bonnett, who *really* pushed me
to write at a professional level about the natural world;
and Richard "Dick" Morton, who always inspired me
by bestowing such high praise upon my work.

CONTENTS

ACKNOWLEDGMENTS

I want to express my deepest appreciation to my husband, Robert, without whose support I could never have come this far, and to my Mom-in-law, Barbara Butler, who patiently waited for the day my book would be finished so she could see me again! I am extremely grateful to Dr. Gregory Degnan of the University of Virginia Health System Department of Orthopaedic Surgery, under whose care I have been able to continue to take photographs and to make notes about my wildlife observations. I am also deeply indebted to Dr. William Dandridge, Jr., Dr. Robert L. Stokes, Jr., and their entire staff for managing my overall health care with a superabundance of compassion and kindness. My thanks to The Camera Center, Cary's Camera Center, and Stubblefield's (especially to Coe Sweet) of Charlottesville, Virginia, for the care they have shown my film and the helpful advice they have given me regarding photography. I am indebted to Pro Camera for help in procuring camera accessories and for photographic equipment repairs. I would like to thank Virginia Glass of Charlottesville for providing me with quality windows through which to watch and photograph wildlife. I am grateful to the staff of the *The Daily Progress* (especially Anita Shelburne and Pat Alther) for giving me the opportunity to write my first newspaper column and to Spike Knuth and Lee Walker of the Virginia Department of Game and Inland Fisheries for giving me the chance to write my first monthly magazine column, in *Virginia Wildlife*. And my sincere gratitude to Jim Condon, who bought me my first computer (along with a program to teach me how to type!) and my first "real" camera with an excellent lens to capture the wildlife that I love so very much.

INTRODUCTION

Do you believe that wildlife and gardens are compatible? Unfortunately, the majority of people who garden have been led to believe that growing plants successfully can only be done at the expense of the natural world. They presume that wildlife is neither wanted nor needed, and they declare war—quite often of the chemical kind—on invading plants and "pests." But war is always stressful, not to mention dangerous. It is not pleasant to be constantly worrying about your cultivated plants, and most pesticides can be as troublesome to people as they are to other organisms.

My yard (which is probably less than half an acre in size) is different from the typical lawn that has just a few shrubs, trees, and flowers. The average grass-filled yard supports very little wildlife, which makes it prone to a host of problems. (It is also quite boring, in my opinion. A yard without much wildlife is a yard without much action!) I have always encouraged wildlife to coexist with me wherever I have lived, and—contrary to what you might expect—I have been able to grow more than enough fruits and vegetables for eating and preserving.

The mostly unrecognized truth is that our yards and gardens need to function in much the same way as a wilderness area does. A gardener who obeys the laws of the natural world owns a garden that is home to numerous organisms (predators and prey) that keep it functioning properly and trouble-free. I call this "living in agreement with nature."

There are numerous benefits to living in agreement with nature. First and foremost, you can *enjoy* your garden instead of constantly fretting over it. Imagine walking out your door hoping to find a new plant or animal instead of worrying that you will encounter some new problem. The stress of gardening is replaced by the thrill of discovery—and with discovery comes free entertainment.

Many people spend time and money traveling to national parks and federal or state management areas in order to observe wildlife. But by gardening in a more natural manner, you may actually see more wildlife from the comfort of your own home than you ever will in an area where the animals are trying to hide from the crowds.

Two young Eastern Screech-Owls look out of their nesting box in the author's yard a few days before venturing out into the world.

When I tell people that I get to see an owl almost every day, during daylight hours, from fall through spring, they tend to be incredulous. After all, most people have never seen an owl in their lives. You can imagine how folks feel when I add that nearly every spring my yard serves as home to an entire family of owls, affording me the grand opportunity to watch owlets.

But it is not by chance that I am given the opportunity to observe owls; they roost and nest close to my house because of how I manage my yard. When you garden naturally, you create a pesticide-free environment that is safe for wildlife as well as people and pets.

In addition to safety, there are other advantages. When you do not use pesticides, you can eat the fruits (and vegetables) of your labors right off the plants if you so desire—no washing necessary! And, of course, a pesticide-free yard does not contribute toxic substances to the soil and water of your home and to properties nearby and downstream.

Furthermore, living in agreement with nature saves you money by replacing chemical fertilizers with natural ones such as dried stalks and leaves. The natural gardener can also save money by taking advantage of volunteer plants—those that start growing in the yard without having been planted. Naturalized plants often offer just as much beauty for the homeowner (and value for wildlife) as cultivated plants bought from nurseries.

In this book, I share what I have learned about gardening by letting the natural world be my guide. If you want to be a contented gardener by living in agreement with nature, or if you simply want to obtain a better understanding of the natural world, this book has been written for you. Once you learn the principles of natural gardening, you can actually allow your garden to do most of the work for you. And without the threat and dread of combat, you will be able to smile and enjoy your yard and gardening. As you'll see, gardening and wildlife are a natural combination. Welcome to my garden.

Chapter 1

Understanding Natural Processes

Although human beings can alter the natural environment, they cannot overcome the basic processes by which it works. These processes constitute the "laws" of nature, which, when obeyed by gardeners, result in a properly functioning environment and garden. Unfortunately, the typical American yard—mostly lawn, with a few shrubs and trees and perhaps some flowers—is inconsistent with the natural world and therefore cannot function correctly.

In nature, a landscape is composed of numerous kinds of plants in proximity to one another. Sometimes a landscape may appear to have a limited variety of plant life, but a closer look usually reveals a much greater assortment. For example, when you observe roadside vegetation from behind the wheel of a car, only the most obvious plants catch your eye as you drive by. These plants may be noticeable because they are the most numerous and perhaps the tallest. Understandably, you may believe that the plant life is not very diverse and that the plants in plain sight are the only ones growing there. However, if you walked along the same roadway and really looked at the vegetation—especially if you performed this activity throughout the seasons—you could be quite surprised by what you discover.

Within a mile of my home, the roadside vegetation appears to be mostly the same lawn grass that is planted in the yards bordering the road. But a walk along the pavement in early spring reveals many astonishing delights. Native wildflowers—too short to be noticed from a vehicle or even by a jogger—become visible to the keen observer. With

The delightful Dutchman's Breeches is an example of a native wildflower that might be found along roadsides.

descriptive names such as Dutchman's Breeches, Spring Beauty, and Jack-in-the-Pulpit, these wonderful plants are visible only to those who consciously seek them.

The Balance of Nature

The proper functioning of the natural world is accomplished by extremely complex and involved interactions and interdependencies. Yet the basis for these relationships is deceptively simple and can be summarized in just one sentence: *All life exists in a tenuous balance that demands that no one organism increase in number so that it becomes out of proportion or unduly emphasized at the expense of other organisms.* Some people have the mistaken notion that *balance* implies a steady state, where nothing ever changes. But one meaning of *balance* is "to bring elements into harmony." And to accomplish harmony, the different elements must be *arranged* so that they form a well-proportioned whole. Arranging denotes taking action, so the balance of nature is actually a system full of action—where organisms are being arranged, or managed, to create an overall harmony.

If you examine the system closely, you can see that the many parts—the organisms—are in a state of continuous change. But if you look at the system from a distance, you will see the sum of the parts functioning as a whole in overall balance—unless something is out of whack.

If your garden is allowed to function as the real world does, any particular kind of organism that becomes too numerous will be dealt a blow by other organisms. Indeed, the world must work in this manner, and the laws of nature must be followed. If you disregard the laws of nature and try to take matters into your own hands, it will rarely, if ever, work out well—for either you or the natural world.

Natural Interactions and Interdependencies

When you think about gardening, the first type of organism (other than plants) that comes to mind is the insect. Insects are plentiful in terms of both variety (species) and total numbers. Sadly, many people dislike insects and are often afraid of them. Of course, insects that bite or sting require respect and should be given a wide berth. However, fear of all insects is not rational.

As a child, I had an insect phobia. I was absolutely terrified of these seemingly otherworldly creatures. If any kind of insect landed on me, I immediately jumped, a shiver ran through me, and my heart raced uncontrollably. This made it quite difficult for me to enjoy being outside. But it was my love of the outside and my desire to explore the natural world that forced me to deal with my phobia. I decided to learn all I could about insects, and to my surprise, with that knowledge came understanding and less fear. I am now able to be around insects—although I still prefer that they land on someone else!

The benefit of having gotten past my phobia is that I now understand how ignorance (and the fear that results from it) can cause folks to kill innocent creatures unnecessarily. I might have done the same if I had not had such a keen love of nature. It is absolutely crucial that you learn about the natural world so you can deal with it rationally. Insects are extremely important to the proper functioning of our planet and we humans could not possibly exist without them. Thus, our attitude should be one of gratitude instead of fear or hatred.

One essential function that insects perform is the pollination, or fertilization, of plants so that they can reproduce by way of seeds. Without pollinators such as bees, butterflies, and wasps, we would not be able to enjoy the many kinds of fruits and vegetables available to us—courtesy of the efforts of insects. In fact, growers who use pesticides kill so many native insects that they must "import" pollinators: they pay beekeepers to bring honeybee hives to their orchards and farms to pollinate their plants. However, over the past two decades, two kinds of Asian parasitic mites have devastated honeybee populations, creating a serious problem for growers. This is one example of how humans without an understanding of the natural world bring problems upon themselves.

Huge farms and orchards that consist of too many acres of one crop are called monocultures and are an obvious invitation to the hordes of insects that naturally feed upon the plants being grown. To battle this problem, growers nonselectively exterminate most of the insects around their growing areas—in the process, wiping out a wide variety of insects and other wildlife necessary for the proper functioning of the environment. (Monocultures exist in the natural world, but not to the extent of human invention.)

People may think that insects "want" to kill their highly prized plants. However, healthy plants are not normally bothered by moderate numbers of insects feeding upon them. If you have a plant that has attracted an abundance of insects that seem to be weakening it, the plant probably has an environmental problem that needs to be addressed, or your yard is not home to the predators necessary to keep those particular insects in check.

People often assume that the appearance of a large group of unidentified insects on a plant must be "bad." They automatically think that the plant is "infested" and will be harmed. Thus their first instinct is to kill the insects. Instead, folks should take the time to identify the little creatures and understand their function. Everything has a purpose in the natural world.

For instance, if you grow Common Milkweed to attract Monarch butterflies (female Monarchs lay their eggs on milkweed because that is what the hatching caterpillars feed on), you are likely to find Large Milk-

This Large Milkweed Bug and its young serve as a natural herbicide, feeding upon milkweed seeds and killing them, thus reducing the number of "volunteer" seedlings the following year.

weed Bug adults and nymphs (young insects that look similar to adults but are smaller and not yet sexually mature). These insects normally cluster on milkweed seedpods, where they suck the juice from developing or fully formed seeds. Each milkweed seedpod holds a few hundred seeds, each of which could germinate—turning your yard into a milkweed patch. A seed sucked dry of its juice, however, cannot germinate. Thus, Large Milkweed Bugs destroy hundreds of seeds, and if you kill them, you wipe out what is effectively a natural herbicide. If you let nature take its course, the number of milkweed seeds that germinate and produce seedlings will be limited naturally, so you will not have to expend energy pulling out as many unwanted plants or use herbicides to kill seedlings.

There are many such organisms whose role is to limit plant production, either by restricting the number of seeds that survive (as accomplished by Large Milkweed Bugs) or by preventing plants from flowering (as occurs when deer eat certain plants). In the natural world, plants must be kept in check. The number of individuals of any one species has to be restricted because of the physical limitations of the Earth; there is simply not enough room on the planet for every seed to become a plant. The amount of physical space allotted to each organism must be restricted due to the variety of life-forms required for the environment to function properly. If any one organism increases beyond its natural boundaries, it will crowd other organisms, whose functions are then impacted. The result is a chain reaction of problems, with the entire equilibrium of nature being thrown off balance. Therefore, it pays to understand the function of insects and other creatures in your yard and garden.

One type of plant-eating animal that is particularly and inappropriately disliked by gardeners is the caterpillar. People think of it as a plant destroyer. Caterpillars usually eat leaves, which plants depend upon to make food. But destroying plants is not the function of a caterpillar; its function is to serve as an important food source for many other kinds of animals. If you think about it, it makes no sense for a caterpillar to eat its food source to death. That would be illogical, because plants that do not get the chance to reproduce do not provide food for the next generation of caterpillars.

Consider again the Monarch butterfly. Because its caterpillar feeds only upon various species of milkweed, it is important to the survival of future generations of Monarchs that milkweed plants survive long enough to reproduce. If a milkweed plant is destroyed by caterpillars, something is out of whack. The problem may be that there were too few

It is unfortunate that so many gardeners dislike caterpillars. Some, such as this Laurel Sphinx Moth, can be quite attractive.

milkweed plants to allow the female Monarchs to spread their eggs around. For example, in an area with many milkweed plants available, a female will lay only one or perhaps a few eggs per plant. At six feet tall, a mature Common Milkweed can easily feed a few caterpillars and still continue to grow, putting out new leaves and flowers and producing seeds.

A plant with too many caterpillars could also be a sign that there are too few predators in your yard. Animals usually produce enough young to keep the species going in spite of some predation and other mortality risk factors (discussed in more detail in chapter 6). It is only natural for some of the caterpillars to be killed; otherwise, there may be too many on one plant for it to feed all of them without suffering irreversible harm.

Irreversible harm can also be a sign that the affected plant is already sickly or under stress, usually because of environmental conditions that make it difficult for the plant to survive. When a plant is in a weakened state, it attracts organisms whose function may be to hurry the process along. In the big picture, a weak or sickly plant is unlikely to reproduce, so it is taking up valuable space. The sooner such a plant dies, the sooner a robust plant can take its place. But if this plant is in your garden, you may not want it to die. And if you have encouraged lots of wildlife to live in your area, help may be on the way.

For example, I grow Perennial Pea vines that invariably suffer from a lack of water during the hot Virginia summers. As a result, they become hosts to a large number of aphids. The weakened plants become visibly distressed—the vines display shriveled but living green leaves and browning dead leaves. Attracted by these visual cues, American Goldfinches fly to the vines to feed on the aphids. Once a goldfinch has visited an ailing pea plant and discovered aphids on it, the bird will be drawn to such a plant whenever it wants to eat insects. (Although American Goldfinches eat mostly seeds, they sometimes eat insects for nutrition. While the goldfinches are making a meal of the aphids to keep themselves alive, they are undoubtedly helping to keep my vines alive too. By removing the juice-sucking aphids, the goldfinches reduce the rate of dehydration, and the plants are able to survive the dry, hot conditions. Indeed, I have never lost even one Perennial Pea vine. As soon as rain arrives, the vines recover nicely, as if there had never been a problem. And in this particular case, I avoid having to draw precious and limited groundwater from my well to keep my plants alive.

Thus, insects play many roles in the natural world, including those of pollinator, seed destroyer, and prey. And of course, numerous other kinds of wildlife are simultaneously interacting with insects, as well as with plants and one another.

Spiders, although commonly thought of as insects, are actually arachnids. Arachnids have eight legs (insects have six) and only two main body parts (insects have three). Spiders are crucial to the natural world as both predators and prey. Some arachnids—such as daddy-long-legs, which are related to but are not technically spiders—feed upon dead animals, making them important as scavengers. Scavengers help to recycle nutrients from dead creatures back into the environment.

A daddy-long-legs in its role as scavenger, feeding upon a dead European Hornet (a scary-looking but non-aggressive wasp).

Although many folks are afraid of spiders, they still think of these eight-legged critters as "good" because they feed upon insects, which are often considered "bad." However, there are no "good" or "bad" species of wildlife. Every animal exists to fulfill a role.

Many species of wasps help to limit spider numbers. Spider wasps paralyze at least one spider for each wasp larva to feed upon after hatching from its egg.

Slugs are crucial to the proper functioning of the environment. They recycle dead animals and plants for the benefit of those that are living.

Arachnid populations are controlled by other arachnids as well as by many other creatures, such as insects and birds. For example, numerous species of wasps provision their nests with paralyzed spiders; when the eggs hatch, the larvae have fresh food to eat. Adult birds also feed large numbers of spiders to their chicks.

Other kinds of invertebrates that are often considered troublesome in the garden are slugs and snails. People may use potent pesticides to poison these animals, or they may put out "beer traps" (when the animals try to reach the beer, they fall into it and drown). But slugs and snails are actually critical to the proper functioning of the home landscape. These unusual-looking creatures usually perform as scavengers, feeding upon and thus recycling plant debris and the carcasses of animals. Slugs and snails are therefore helping to fertilize your plants. When they break down plant and animal matter into its smaller components and release these as part of their wastes, they are returning nutrients to the environment. Earthworms may feed upon the snail and slug wastes, incorporating the nutrients into the soil by way of their own excrement, called soil castings.

If snails and slugs become too numerous and are in need of food, they may turn to the gardener's plants to avoid starvation. (A desperate animal will feed upon anything it can ingest, even if it may not be able to actually digest the substance available). A gardener who is experiencing a problem with snails and slugs in all likelihood has a garden that is too wet. Overly moist areas typically have lots of decaying organic matter (such as mulch) for these animals to eat. In addition, the gardener probably has not encouraged snail and slug predators to coexist by providing good habitat for them.

Firefly larvae often wander far from their mossy maternity ward, helping to limit slug and snail populations all around the natural gardener's yard.

The larvae of lightning bugs (or fireflies) are prime predators of snails and slugs. Lightning bugs lay their eggs in moss because it tends to stay damp; this prevents the eggs from drying out, which would be lethal to the developing animals inside. Yet many people eradicate moss from their yards. With no moss in the yard, lightning bugs will not lay their eggs, so there will be no larvae to control the snail and slug populations.

Preventing moss from growing leads to insect overpopulations as well. Birds, which are prime predators of caterpillars, aphids, and other insects, may need moss to make their nests. For example, the most abundant material in a chickadee nest is moss. Therefore, you can put up a chickadee nest box, but if you do not encourage a patch of moss to grow in your yard, the chickadees will probably nest elsewhere.

A Carolina Chickadee pair will nest in a box, but only if moss is available nearby.

The natural world is full of such interactions taking place daily around you. Yet they often go unnoticed and may be prevented from occurring if you do not allow nature to take its course. You should now be able to understand why it is best to treat your yard as a minuscule fragment of the natural world. By using the natural world as your model and incorporating the many kinds of plants and animals that exist in nature, you will encourage the numerous interactions that are the true "secrets" of the garden.

Chapter 2

Planning Your Garden

Any location that is suitable for growing plants can become a nature-friendly garden. It is not difficult to create the appropriate habitat in a yard around a house, on the rooftop of a city building, on the balcony of an apartment, outside a school or library, on farmland, along unused strips of land at airports, around golf courses, and on the premises of many kinds of businesses. The basic principles are the same, no matter how big or how small your garden is going to be.

Analyzing the Basics

The first step is to limit the amount of lawn grass. Lawns are great for people to walk on and for children to play on, but they do not provide much food, cover, or nesting spots for wildlife. Lawns also require a lot of maintenance that can have secondary effects that are harmful to the environment. Lawn mower exhaust pollutes the air, and runoff from chemical fertilizers and pesticides can contaminate local waterways and even reach the sea, creating serious problems for life-forms hundreds of miles away. Decide how much lawn to get rid of by determining which areas you want to make nature friendly. Envision flowers, vines, shrubs, and trees growing around the edges of the yard or as focal points within the yard.

11

Next, draw a diagram of the various gardens you intend to create. Measure the size of the different garden areas and draw them to scale and in approximately the correct shape to estimate how many plants you will need. Note the amount of sunlight different areas get, the soil conditions, and whether there are any structures that will have an effect upon nearby plants. You can then decide what kinds of plants to grow in each area, based on their cultivation requirements.

The next step is to have your garden soil tested by a local extension office or perhaps through a university. Some garden centers accept soil samples that they will send out to be tested, for a fee. You may want to provide one soil sample from each area of the yard that you plan to landscape. Soil conditions can vary quite a bit from one place to another, even within just a few feet. For example, my mother-in-law has three hollies of the same species that were planted at the same time in a row and have always been treated the same. One plant is big and robust, the one next to it is not quite as vigorous, and the third plant is a bit of a runt. This variable outcome is undoubtedly due to differing soil conditions.

When you send in a soil sample, you may be asked what kinds of plants you intend to grow. After the analysis, the agent can recommend how to alter the soil if it does not meet the requirements of the plants you wish to grow.

A soil analysis consists of determining the pH (acidic, alkaline, or neutral), soil type (clayey, sandy, or loamy—a clue to the amount of organic matter present), and soil texture (size of the individual soil particles, which indicates how well the soil will hold water). You may also be informed of plant nutrients that are underrepresented or overly abundant.

You can buy an inexpensive kit and test the soil pH yourself. One drawback, however, is that you will not know the proper amounts of soil additives to use to alter pH or nutrients. It might be best to obtain a professional soil analysis and then perform your own analysis periodically to check the pH. Maintaining the proper pH is crucial to plant nutrition because it determines how well a plant can absorb nutrients through its roots.

You can determine soil type and texture by squeezing some moist (not wet) soil in your hand. The soil is clayey if it sticks together when you squeeze it, sandy if it runs out of your hand, and loamy if it sticks together only slightly. (Loamy soil also has a dark color.) Clayey and sandy soils tend to be low in organic matter, but loamy soils are wonderfully full of this material. Due to the tiny size of the individual soil particles, clay soil tends to stick together, holding moisture and being slow to drain. Sandy soil is composed of large particles that water runs through quickly; thus it tends to dry out very fast. Loamy soil is the best; it holds water just long enough for most plants to grow well without rotting.

If you are planning to grow plants in containers on your balcony, rooftop, patio, porch, or deck, soil conditions are not a problem. Many stores sell potting soil that is already at the proper pH and has the right texture for container gardening.

The growing season in most of the United States begins in spring and runs through fall, up until the first frost. From late spring until early summer, the sun is close to its highest elevation above the horizon. This is the time to determine whether the various locations of your garden receive "full sun" (at least six to eight hours of sunlight a day) or not (less than six hours a day). Unless you are already quite familiar with your garden site, you will need to study the area for several days or longer, until you feel confident that you know how many hours of direct sunlight each spot gets daily during most of the growing season.

Another site consideration is the direction and duration of prevailing winds. Moving air tends to dry out plants and can affect how cold or hot a spot is. Nearby structures can also create such microclimates. For example, a brick wall absorbs heat during the day and releases it at night. Any nearby plants might get too hot during the heat of summer to survive, or, contrarily, they may be able to survive an unusually cold winter with the help of the heat given off by the brick wall.

After you have made a note of all these factors on your drawings, the fun part begins: determining exactly what plants you are going to grow.

Attracting Wildlife

If you are turning a yard or a fair amount of land into a wildlife refuge, you can grow many different plants to attract an assortment of animals. But if your space is limited, the variety of wildlife you will be able to host in your nature-friendly garden will also be limited.

Some people wish to attract butterflies, some folks want to bring in songbirds, and still others would like to draw hummingbirds. To do so requires that you learn the needs of the particular animals you have in mind and what kinds of plants can accommodate those needs. However, try as you might, you cannot garden only for particular animals.

For example, when you grow nectar plants for butterflies and hummingbirds, you will also attract moths, wasps, bees, and many other

This White-lined Sphinx Moth was feeding at Touch-me-nots along the author's porch. However, it undoubtedly was in the area due to the presence of Four o'clock plants, one of the host plants for its caterpillars.

In a yard that is functioning naturally, caterpillar numbers are controlled by butterfly and moth mortality. Here, a crab spider has caught a Spicebush Swallowtail on the author's Lantana.

kinds of insects. Spiders will probably arrive to feed upon many of these insects. If the nectar plants happen to be food plants for some species of moths and butterflies, you may have caterpillars feeding on them, which will attract predators such as birds. In addition, deer may be especially attracted to some of the plants in your garden. You need to accept that all of these creatures are part of your world and include them in your garden planning.

You can learn to recognize the plants that provide food, protection, and nesting sites for various kinds of wildlife by enjoying a "wildlife walk." Take time to observe your surroundings and make notes about what you see.

Robber flies may look menacing to humans, but they are only a threat to flying insects like this hapless moth, which was captured in the author's garden.

If you live in a rural area, take a stroll along country roads during spring or summer. Look closely at the wildflowers, vines, shrubs, and trees. If you live in an urban or sub-urban area, walk down streets where residents have planted flower gardens or shrubs and trees near the sidewalks. And no matter where you live, there is probably a park or even a public garden in the vicinity that you could visit to make these observations.

You are looking for signs of use by wildlife. If you see a flower that has a variety of insects feeding on its nectar, whether it is an herbaceous plant or a woody tree or shrub, you will know that it is a great plant for wildlife. Hummingbirds also assist in this important activity. Plants that attract many kinds of insects also lure predators. Spiders, robber flies, dragonflies, and birds—all insect predators—will hunt for meals among such flowers.

During fall and winter, take another wildlife walk to look for plants with seeds or fruits. These may be useful foods for other forms of wildlife, such as birds and small mammals.

When you discover a plant that has attracted wildlife and you think that it might grow well on your piece of real estate, make a note of its name and its growing conditions. If you do not know the name of the plant, you will need to identify it. Carrying a camera along on your walks is a great way to record potential plants for your garden, especially if you do not know their names. Always photograph the stem and leaves as well as the flowers. This will be helpful in identifying the mystery plants using a field guide. Field guides for plants growing in different regions of the United States are available at bookstores and libraries. If you have difficulty making the identifications, bring the photos to a local plant expert for help. Nature and garden clubs have folks who are knowledgeable about plants and will be happy to assist you. Or, if the plants are located in a garden, simply ask the gardener what they are.

Evergreen plants are wonderful for nesting sites and shelter in the harsh winter, and they offer protection from predators year-round. Deciduous shrubs and trees that have lots of foliage during the summer months are employed by wildlife as well. Thick tangles of vines are often used by birds and small mammals for roosting or nesting. Even some reptiles and amphibians, such as snakes and treefrogs, rest on the branches of shrubs and small trees during the day.

Any plant whose branches grow close enough together to block the line of sight to the trunk is a likely shelter for wildlife. You can confirm wildlife use by being observant on your wildlife walks. During summer, watch for birds flying into plant growth and staying put for several minutes. During the winter, after the leaves have fallen, look for old stick or leaf nests among the branches.

Modifying the Landscape

Once you have made a list of good wildlife plants for your area, study the notes you made on your diagram. You will need to match the plants to the environment you can provide for them. For instance, a plant that needs full shade (eight hours or more a day) will die if it is placed in full sun.

No matter what your landscape is like right now, it is possible to modify it for the use of wildlife. A shady yard, much like the interior of a forest, does not provide a lot of food and therefore will have the smallest variety of creatures. However, even a shady lot can be improved for wildlife by growing shade-loving plants that produce fruits or seeds. A sunny or partly sunny yard gives you more choices, though, because most flowering and fruit-bearing plants need full sun. A yard that receives full sun, much like a field, can produce a lot of food and will attract quite an assortment of animals. A yard that is mostly sunny but also has boundaries of large shrubs and trees, much like a field surrounded by forest, offers both food and cover and thus will support the largest variety of critters.

Where field meets woods is known as edge habitat. Your goal is to mimic such conditions, which is accomplished by creating three levels of plant life. The shortest level consists of grasses and flowers. These plants furnish food, but they can also supply cover, nesting materials, and nest sites. For example, caterpillars and rabbits are consumers of the fresh green parts of plants, while butterflies and other insects slurp nectar from the flowers, and songbirds and small mammals eat the seeds that

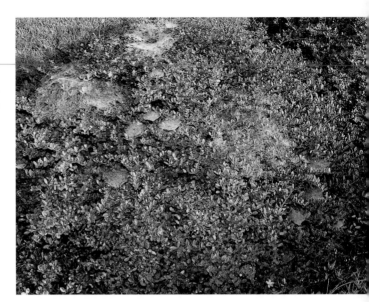

Some folks remove spider webbing from their plants because they think it looks too messy. If you leave the webbing on the plant, however, it will provide day-and-night insect protection.

are formed later. If you can grow some tall native grasses (not lawn grass), animals will be able to hide among the stems for protection from predators, and if the grassy area is large enough, ground-nesting birds, such as meadowlarks, will be able to reproduce.

The middle level of a wildlife habitat consists of thick vines (known as thickets or tangles when they occur naturally) or densely growing shrubs. This layer of growth reaches a minimum of five or six feet tall to a maximum of about twelve to fifteen feet. Most species of songbirds nest within this height range. Vines and shrubs also provide food for wildlife. The right species of shrubs, such as viburnums and hollies, produce fruit for summer, fall, or winter nourishment. Many vines possess nectar-rich flowers for summer hummingbirds. Later, fruit or seedpods develop for the benefit of seed- and fruit-eating birds and small mammals during autumn and winter.

Trees constitute the third and tallest level of the wildlife garden. But do not be dismayed if your yard is too small to grow large trees. There are many smaller trees that serve the intended function just as well. Trees provide shade for relief from hot summer sunshine; they provide food for wildlife; and, if they are at least fifteen to twenty feet tall, they provide nesting sites for those creatures that prefer to be higher off the ground.

You can also provide shelter and nesting sites for wildlife by making brush piles. Gardeners sometimes have to trim shrubs and trees or even

Many kinds of wildlife make use of brush piles. Birds and mammals may nest or take shelter from predators within them. Sowbugs and other invertebrates will help recycle the decaying wood, attracting salamanders and lizards that will feed upon them.

remove them. Rather than letting these cuttings go to waste by burning them or carting them away, pile them up in a corner of the yard or out in a field, where the interlocking branches will provide refuge for small animals. As the plant material begins to decay, it will create the proper habitat for lizards and salamanders to lay their eggs. Some of these cold-blooded animals may even hibernate at the bottom of a brush pile. Eventually, the brush pile will decay into rich compost that you can use in your garden plots. If you are afraid the brush pile will look too messy, grow vines over it (they can be trained to go up over the pile) or hide it behind a screen of shrubbery.

Many animals require dead trees to nest and take shelter in. If you leave these standing on your property, many kinds of mammals (squirrels, bats, opossums), birds (woodpeckers, wood ducks, owls), and insects (overwintering butterflies) will make use of them.

Many folks feed birds by putting out store-bought seeds (see chapter 4), but a better way to provide food is via your wildlife plantings. If you can grow a variety of plants so that seeds and fruits are available year-round, it will be easier for both you and the birds. Then, even if you are not home, the birds will be provided for. And you will not feel obligated to trudge out to the feeder during a snowstorm if the birds can find food in your wildlife garden. Therefore, when planning your garden, grow a variety of plants whose fruits or seeds ripen from early spring to fall. Some late-bearing plants will hold on to their fruits and seeds well into winter, which is extremely important because this is the most difficult time of year for all animals to find food.

All properties are different, so you have the opportunity to create a unique garden full of wildlife. If you are unsure about which plants to grow, contact the resources listed in the back of the book for more specific information. Once you finalize your plans, you are ready to create a wildlife garden that will allow you to live in agreement with nature.

Let your flowers go to seed and leave your dried flower stalks standing to provide food for birds and small mammals. As soon as new growth starts to show in early spring, cut down the stalks and leave them where they fall to nourish your plants as they decay.

PLANTS THAT ATTRACT WILDLIFE

Note: Some of the plants in this listing may be considered "invasive" in your area. Please see Chapter 3 for a discussion of this issue.

Abelia: flowering shrub used by hummingbirds, butterflies, moths, bees, and other insects but not bothered by deer

Achillea millefolium (Yarrow): flower (usually white) used by butterflies and other insects; songbirds eat the seeds

Aesculus parviflora (Bottlebrush Buckeye): flowering shrub used by hummingbirds, butterflies, and other insects but not bothered by deer

Ageratum houstonianum: flower visited by insects; birds (especially goldfinches and juncos) eat the seeds

Albizia julibrissin (Mimosa or Silk Tree): flowering tree; a super attractant to hummingbirds

Amelanchier (Serviceberry or Shadbush): shrub or small tree; flowers attract insects; fruits extremely popular with birds and mammals (including humans); not bothered by deer

Asclepias (milkweed): native flowers highly attractive to butterflies and bees; larval food plant of Monarch butterflies, but *Asclepias tuberosa* (Butterfly Weed) may cause Monarchs to be more palatable to predators; easiest species to find may be *Asclepias syriaca* (Common Milkweed)

Asimina triloba (Pawpaw): small tree; sole larval food plant of the Zebra Swallowtail butterfly

Aster: many species of native late fall-blooming flowers that serve as an important food source at this time of the year for late-flying butterflies (especially migrating Monarchs) and other insects; birds take seeds; larval food plants of several species of crescent butterflies

Boehmeria cylindrica (False Nettle): native flower; food plant of Red Admiral, Question Mark, Eastern Comma butterflies; birds take seeds

Buddleia (Butterfly Bush): shrub with flowers that attract insects, especially butterflies and moths

Campsis radicans (Trumpet Creeper): native vine with tubular flowers; especially attracts hummingbirds and black ants, as well as some species of moths; seeds attract goldfinches, titmice, chickadees, juncos, and small mammals

Celosia: fertilized flowers attractive to insects; seeds taken by many species of seed-eating birds

Cercis canadensis (Eastern Redbud): small native tree that blooms early to the delight of recently emerged bees and other insects

Cichorium intybus (Chicory): beautiful flower provides nectar and pollen for insects; seeds eaten by birds

Cleome spinosa (Spiderflower): flower attracts insects and humming-birds; seeds are taken by birds, especially Mourning Doves

Coreopsis lanceolata (Lance-leaved Coreopsis): yellow flower attractive to insects; seeds eagerly taken by American Goldfinches and Dark-eyed Juncos

Cornus florida (Flowering Dogwood): small native tree; provides berries attractive to birds, especially Eastern Bluebirds; a larval food plant of Spring Azure butterfly

Cosmos: flowers attractive to insects; green seeds eaten by American Goldfinches; mature seeds attractive to White-throated Sparrows, Dark-eyed Juncos, and House Finches

Daucus carota (Queen Anne's Lace): flower attracts bumblebees, butter-flies, and other insects; larval food plant of Black Swallowtail butterfly

Elaeagnus umbellatus (Autumn Olive) or *angustifolia* (Russian Olive): shrub or tree provides nesting sites for birds; flowers attract insects; berries eagerly taken by birds and mammals, including American Black Bears; not bothered by deer

Euonymus alata (Winged Euonymus): shrub provides nesting sites for birds; flowers attract insects; early-fall fruits eaten by Northern Cardinals, Eastern Bluebirds, and White-throated Sparrows

Eupatorium (Boneset, Snakeroot, Joe-Pye-weed): native flowers extremely attractive to insects and hummingbirds; birds eagerly eat seeds; not bothered by deer

Fuchsia triphylla (Honeysuckle Fuchsia): attractive to hummingbirds; easy to grow in a pot; good for areas with partial sun

Helianthus (sunflower): flower attracts insects; birds and mammals eagerly feed on seeds

Hemerocallis fulva (daylily): flower attractive to hummingbirds and insects; unfortunately, a deer delicacy

Hesperis matronalis (Dame's Rocket): flower attracts insects; seeds attract songbirds; not bothered by deer

Hosta (Plantain Lily): flower attracts hummingbirds; one of the few shade-loving wildlife plants

Ilex (hollies): shrubs or trees; flowers attractive to insects; fruits useful as a mid- to late-winter food source for birds

Impatiens capensis (Jewelweed or Touch-me-not): flower used by insects and birds; Black Bears eat juicy stems

Ipomoea purpurea (Morning Glory) or *quamoclit pennata* (Cypress Vine) or *quamoclit x multifada* (Cardinal Climber): flowers are especially attractive to hummingbirds and day-flying moths; Dark-eyed Juncos and Northern Cardinals eat seeds

Juniperus (junipers): evergreen trees and shrubs provide nesting and roosting sites for birds; fruits eaten by birds and mammals

Kniphofia (Red Hot Poker): flower attractive to hummingbirds; seeds taken by House Finches; not bothered by deer

Lantana camara: woody flowering plant that provides much nectar for insects and hummingbirds; can be grown in pot, then cut back and overwintered inside; not bothered by deer

Lathyrus (pea family): flowering vines that are attractive to insects and hummingbirds; American Goldfinches pick aphids off vines during dry spells

Ligustrum (privet): shrub flowers especially attractive to butterflies and bees; fruits are a good late-winter food source for birds and small mammals; not bothered by deer

Lobelia cardinalis (Cardinal Flower): flower that is very attractive to hummingbirds, sphinx moths, bumblebees

Lonicera sempervirens (Trumpet Honeysuckle) or *japonica* (Japanese Honeysuckle): native flowering vine (Trumpet) or nonnative shrub or vine (Japanese); hummingbirds and insects come to blooms; fruit is eaten by songbirds and mammals

Mentha (mints): flowers very attractive to insects, especially bees and butterflies

Mirabilis jalapa (Four-o'clock or Marvel-of-Peru): flower very attractive to insects and hummingbirds; seeds taken by birds; larval food plant of White-lined Sphinx Moth

Monarda didyma (Bee Balm) or *fistulosa* (Wild Bergamot): native flowers of the mint family attractive to hummingbirds (Bee Balm) and insects (Wild Bergamot); seeds attractive to songbirds; not bothered by deer

Nicotiana alata (Flowering Tobacco): flower opens late in day; used by hummingbirds and sphinx moths

Ocimum basilicum (Purple Ruffles): flowering herb very attractive to insects; seeds eagerly taken by American Goldfinches and Dark-eyed Juncos

Oenothera biennis (Common Evening Primrose) or *speciosa* (Showy Evening Primrose): night-opening flower (Common Evening) especially attractive to sphinx moths; day-opening flower (Showy Evening) attractive to bees, hummingbirds, and hummingbird moths; seeds eagerly taken by many species of birds

Parthenocissus quinquefolia (Virginia Creeper) or *tricuspidata* (Boston Ivy): vines that attract insects to blooms; birds and mammals to fruits

Passiflora: vines are larval food plants of Variegated Fritillary and other butterflies

Phlox: flowers popular with hummingbirds and insects, as well as deer

Photinia serrulata (Redtips): evergreen shrub that, if allowed to grow naturally to its full height, provides nesting and roosting sites for birds; red fruits during late fall and early winter attractive to birds (American Robins, Cedar Waxwings) and mammals

Pyrus calleryana 'Bradford' (Bradford Pear): tree; flowers attractive to insects; fruits taken by birds and mammals

Rhododendron (Azalea, Rhododendron): flowering shrubs attractive to hummingbirds and insects

Rhus copallina (Shining Sumac) or *typhina* (Staghorn): flowers attractive to insects and fruits attractive to birds

Rudbeckia hirta (Black-eyed Susan) or *speciosa* (Showy Coneflower): attractive to insects; seeds taken by songbirds; not bothered by deer

Salvia (sages): produce flowers full of nectar for hummingbirds and insects; seeds for songbirds

Sambucus canadensis (Elderberry): shrub that produces loads of fruit for birds and mammals in late summer; unfortunately, it's "deer candy"

Sassafras albidum (Sassafras): small tree; flowers attract insects; fruits attract birds and mammals, including Black Bears; a larval food plant of Spicebush Swallowtail butterfly and Promethea moth

Silene cucubalus (Bladder Campion): nonnative wildflower attractive to hummingbirds and many kinds of insects

Solidago (goldenrods): native flowers extremely useful to insects, especially migrating Monarch butterflies, in autumn; seeds taken by songbirds

Sorbus (Mountain Ash): trees that provide flowers for insects and fruits for birds

Tagetes (marigold): flower sometimes attractive to insects; seeds taken by birds; Dainty Marietta (*Tagetes patula nana*) excellent for butterflies

Taraxacum officinale (Common Dandelion): flower that is important nectar source for earliest insects of spring as well as late-flying insects (including Monarch butterflies) of fall; seeds are taken by finches; leaves loved by bunnies

Trifolium (clover): flowers attractive to insects; leaves loved by bunnies

Verbena hortensis: flowers attract many insects and hummingbirds

Vernonia noveboracensis (New York Ironweed): flowers very attractive to butterflies; seeds eagerly taken by birds

Viburnum: flowering shrubs attract insects to blooms and birds and mammals to fruits; avoid non-fruiting viburnums, such as Snowball (*Viburnum opulus roseum* or *Viburnum opulus sterile*)

Viola (violets): native flowers that are the sole larval food sources for many species of fritillary butterflies

Weigela: flowering shrubs attract hummingbirds and insects

Zinnia elegans: flower attractive to hummingbirds and insects; seeds attractive to songbirds

(Note: Always avoid double-flowering varieties; it is hard for animals to get to their nectar. All native trees, shrubs, and herbaceous plants possess wildlife value. Cultivars often lack nectar, fruits, or seeds. Many naturalized plants also provide for wildlife.)

Chapter 3

Allowing Your Garden to Work for You

In order to be a happy gardener, you may have to change your gardening philosophy. Instead of thinking of your yard as an artificial environment to be kept neat and tidy with blemish-free plants, you must recognize that your yard is a part of the natural world, where a completely pristine appearance is impossible to attain. You may want your yard to resemble those ideal gardens depicted in magazines and books, but those lovely photographs represent only a momentary glimpse of what a particular garden looks like. That beauty is fleeting; no garden view is static.

Flowers fade, shrivel, and turn brown. Some plants stop blooming and go dormant, their foliage yellowing and browning, until the plants seem to wilt out of existence. At the end of the growing season, dried stalks may remain where beautiful plants once stood. The look of a garden is always changing, and those changes need to be understood and accepted. When you admit that nature has the upper hand, you can allow your garden to work for you. You will be able to stop fretting about your yard and truly enjoy it.

Accept Natural Processes

Change in the garden is often not happily greeted by gardeners because they find the transformations unattractive. For instance, when spring-blooming bulbs, such as daffodils, finish flowering, people want to cut off the green foliage that remains. They do not want the "leftover" foliage to

The American Goldfinch will feed upon plants that have gone to seed, such as this New York Iron-weed.

crowd the annuals and perennials they have planted to obtain another batch of blooms, nor do they want to see the bulb foliage turn yellow, because they feel that it looks awful. When plants such as Wild Bergamot or Black-eyed Susan are ready to go to seed, people would prefer to cut down the seed stalks instead of allowing them to dry and turn brown. And heaven forbid that leaves should remain underneath the trees that shed them in the fall.

Yet all of these things happen for a reason. The natural world does nothing that is nonsensical. Therefore, if you interfere with these natural processes, you can create problems. It is important to accept the way nature works, and this is easier for those who understand why plants and animals do what they do.

For example, the green leaves that remain after the daffodil has bloomed replenish the bulb's food supply, so that it can bloom again next year. Producing blossoms is an energy-intensive process for a plant. If gardeners do not allow these green leaves to stay put to perform photosynthesis, they deprive the bulbs of the food they need. If the bulbs cannot make enough food, they simply will not bloom the following spring. A lack of blossoms is certainly not the desired outcome, but that is what happens when gardeners interfere with natural processes.

It is accepted horticultural practice to fold bulb leaves and place a rubber band around them, or even to braid the leaves, to get them out of the way. These customs limit photosynthesis, however, because they reduce the leaf surface available to catch the sun's rays. Therefore, tying up a plant's leaves is not very helpful to either the plant or the gardener. If the end result is supposed to be a lovely garden, bundled leaves detract from that beauty (and, I think, they look rather silly).

Many people cut down flower stalks when plants begin to make seeds, in an attempt to prolong the blooming period. But again, the process of creating a flower and then seeds is energy-intensive. By forcing a plant to make more flowers than it "wants to," you are draining the plant of its energy reserves, which could cause it to die over the winter (if it is weakened enough) or to not flower at all the following year. A plant "wants" to produce only a certain number of flower stalks because it "knows" how much food it has stored in its roots. This is why newly planted perennials normally do not bloom until they have been in the ground for a few years. Plants need time to build up their root systems to support top growth.

A plant tries to replace a flower stalk that is cut off (by human or beast) because the whole point of its existence is to reproduce; therefore, it will do its best to accomplish this task no matter how draining the effort is. In the big picture, it is not important if this particular plant dies, as long as it has made numerous seeds to carry on its legacy. Gardeners take advantage of plants' "desire" to reproduce when they cut flower stalks during the growing season, forcing the plant to make more flowers. But knowledgeable gardeners recognize that a plant will naturally produce the optimal number of blooms for its physical condition. They know that by accepting that number, they are helping their plants grow bigger and stronger each year. Plants reward these patient gardeners by increasing the number of blooms they produce in subsequent years.

Plants can obtain nourishment each new growing season from the decomposition of the previous year's flower stalks. When early spring arrives, the dried stems should be cut down and left on the ground, where they will quickly decompose (with the aid of numerous kinds of organisms), enriching the soil. And gardeners who allow flower stalks that have gone to seed to remain standing throughout fall and winter help provide food for birds and small mammals.

Meanwhile, "greedy gardeners" who wanted nonstop blooms will be wondering why their plants are not doing as well as in previous years. They may have to add chemical fertilizer to artificially "pump up" their weakened plants. These impatient gardeners have created work and expense because they did not allow their gardens to work for them.

Limit the Lawn

Lawns are time-consuming, energy-intensive, money-draining projects. Their maintenance requires the use of a limited natural resource (gasoline) that pollutes the air and water, affecting the lives of numerous

A large lawn may look neat and attractive, but it is a drain on the environment, your wallet, and your time.

species of wildlife and the quality of life for humans. Lawns also demand the purchase of equipment—lawn mower, fertilizer spreader, string trimmer—along with gasoline, motor oil, fertilizer (which often contains pesticides), and sometimes lime (or perhaps sulfur) to adjust the pH. Some folks invest in a sprinkler system as well, spending yet more money and increasing the use of another limited natural resource (fresh water). In addition, people have to spend quite a bit of their precious lives cutting the grass, spreading the fertilizer, and raking the leaves so the lawn does not die.

Some lawns are grown so unnaturally thick that they resemble a carpet of Astroturf instead of real grass. Then folks are forced to allot time and money for de-thatching (removing the buildup of matted, dead plant material) and aerating (making holes in the ground to give the roots access to air). When the lawn inevitably becomes diseased due to the overcrowding, the owner then has to invest more time and money applying some product to remedy the situation. But the product invariably treats only the symptom; it does nothing for the root cause (literally) of the problem.

Grass is not meant to be grown in this manner, which is why lawns require so much work to keep them healthy. When plants are packed as tightly as the blades of grass in a carpet of lawn, air cannot circulate to dry them. This constant wetness allows disease organisms and fungi to grow on the grass blades. In short, growing your lawn so that it resembles an artificial carpet is an invitation to continuous work, inevitable problems, and large expenditures.

As if all of this were not bad enough, the small gasoline engines that people use in lawn mowers (and leaf blowers, string trimmers, and so on) spew millions of tons of hydrocarbons, carbon monoxide, and nitrous oxide into the air every year. Everyone who uses a small gasoline engine contributes to our air pollution problem. The gasoline, oil, fertilizers, and pesticides used for lawn care can also run off into local streams and rivers and then on to bays and oceans. This water pollution kills wildlife and impacts human livelihoods dependent on that wildlife.

Instead of growing a lawn with a hugely detrimental impact on your life, other people's lives, and wildlife, it is better to landscape in a manner that imitates the natural world. Keep a lawn (in a more natural state, not as a carpet) only where it will actually be used, either by children playing or adults entertaining, or as pathways for visiting different areas of your yard. Maintain your lawn at the tallest recommended height for your kind of grass. A taller lawn shades the soil, thereby limiting evaporation and conserving ground water. This will also keep your grass green longer into the summer.

Let your entire yard work for you by embracing those plants that do not need pampering to grow well. Allow flowering plants such as clovers, dandelions, and violets to grow in the lawn. Rabbits will probably feed upon the broadleaf plants in the grass instead of your cultivated flowers. Clovers capture nitrogen from the air and add it to the soil, helping your grass to grow better. Dandelions feed numerous kinds of animals, especially in early spring (and late fall, under the right conditions) when not much else is blooming. And violets, in addition to their lovely flowers, will add beauty to your yard in the form of orange-colored fritillary butterflies, which will come to lay eggs on them. By allowing a variety of plants to grow

Some wasps emerge at the slightest hint of warmth, even if the calendar proclaims that it is still winter. The Common Dandelion, which often blooms during the winter and is certainly blooming by the first days of spring, is an important source of nourishment for such insects.

among the grass blades, you will avoid the use of herbicides, which are a danger to people, wildlife, and our waterways.

Use Native and Naturalized Plants

Instead of immediately pulling out any unrecognized seedling that appears in your flower beds, allow it to grow. It just might produce lovely flowers that provide beauty for your family and food for wildlife—absolutely free of expense, time, and maintenance. Many native wildflowers grow well without the help of fertilizers and pesticides, so all you have to do is sit back and enjoy their company. This is also true of many naturalized plants—plants brought to the area by humans, unintentionally or otherwise, that are well adapted to survive in their new "home."

In some areas that lack human management or natural controls, naturalized plants increase to such an extent that they are considered invaders, replacing native plants. Many people consider these types of plants to be "bad" and want them removed from the environment at whatever cost. Common Dandelion is a naturalized plant that many would include on the "invasives" list.

Native plants can also behave in an invasive manner when conditions are perfect for their growth and there is nothing to control or limit their spread. In Virginia, where I live, Trumpet Creeper is often considered an invasive native plant because if it is not managed, it can completely fill an area in several years.

Many "weeds," like this Venus's Looking Glass, are actually beautiful flowers. The patient gardener who allows such plants to mature may be richly rewarded.

However, we should expect plants to spread. The whole point of life for any organism is reproduction. Thus, whether a plant is native or not, its "goal" is to try to increase the numbers of its kind. Plants usually behave in an invasive manner when the environment has somehow been made conducive to their growth and reproduction. For example, in the typical yard and along roadways, most topsoil has been removed and the almost rock-hard subsoil exposed. It takes a tough plant to grow well in subsoil that is neither nutrient-rich nor loosely textured (friable). Luckily for us (because we created these situations), there are plants that can thrive under these conditions—although they are often nonnative species.

English Ivy is a nonnative plant that does well on subsoil.

Nonnative species can help transform subsoil into topsoil that can support native species once again in our yards, along our roadways, and on reclaimed land that was previously a mine or landfill site. Nonnative naturalized species move into these areas free of charge and with no effort on our part, whereas the native plants that people try to replant into these disturbed sites die—a total waste of time, effort, and public monies. Over time, as the soil improves, the nonnative colonizers start to die out, and native species usually become established. But of course, these results can be obtained only if the land is left alone by people.

In areas where the soil is good and wildlife has been encouraged to live, very few plants behave invasively. For instance, I would love to have lots of dandelions in my yard. Yet over the course of twenty years, I have had only a few dandelion plants around my house. The explanation for their scarcity is that I have always landscaped with wildlife in mind, so I have animals that naturally limit the dandelion numbers for me. American Goldfinches relish dandelion seeds, diminishing the total number of seeds available to germinate. In addition, Eastern Cottontail Rabbits feed upon dandelion leaves. If they eat enough of a plant at once, this could delay or eliminate flowering, since defoliated dandelion has to put its energy into growing new leaves.

I also love Trumpet Creeper and intentionally planted it in my yard two decades ago. Its nectar provides food for Ruby-throated Humming-birds, and its seeds are eagerly taken by Dark-eyed Juncos, American Goldfinches, and Gray Squirrels. Its dried, hollow stems are utilized by Tufted Titmice throughout the fall to store sunflower hearts, which the birds can retrieve if food becomes scarce. I have also found caterpillars feeding upon the seeds of Trumpet Creeper inside a seedpod.

Because wildlife uses so many of the seeds, I find very few Trumpet Creeper seedlings in my yard each year. And it is a simple task to pull them out if they take root where I do not want these vines to grow. How-ever, if I did not manage my yard and pull these unwanted seedlings, eventually I would have quite a few Trumpet Creeper plants. At that point, many people would consider this wonderful plant to be invasive, but in actuality, it is not. Very few seedlings come up every year, but most folks pay no attention until there are so many plants that they seem to have suddenly taken over the property.

In more natural areas, such as national parks, forests, and wildlife refuges, plants can also seem invasive because of the same lack of man-agement. But more importantly, these plants usually show up in "natu-ral" areas because land has been disturbed. Park managers create trails

A Gray Squirrel will often eat Trumpet Creeper seeds on the spot, but at other times it will carry the entire pod away to eat later at its nest, espe-cially if the pod is in the green stage.

that, when used heavily, result in compacted soil (making it akin to subsoil). Trails (as well as wildfires) open dark forest interiors to sunlight, making it possible for nonnative sun-loving plants to grow.

It is commonly thought that nonnative "invasive" plants are not utilized by wildlife, but that is simply not true. More often, the problem is that wildlife has not been encouraged or allowed to live in the area.

In terms of the big picture, it is best to grow native plants and embrace—and manage as necessary—naturalized plants that appear on their own. Naturalized plants may actually work better for you and the environment because they are obviously suited to existing growing conditions. If you are concerned about "invasive" plants, avoid buying nonnative plants from nurseries, such as the popular Butterfly Bush, which is native to Asia. This plant grows well in the United States without much help, and as might be expected, it is spreading and may soon be added to the "invasive" plant list.

Let Leaves Lie

Another accepted horticultural practice is to grow grass beneath trees. But how sensible is it to plant something where you know it is going to be smothered by falling leaves every autumn, year in and year out? The grass will die if the leaves are not raked up—another unnecessary chore for you or someone else to perform—yet this foolish custom has become widespread.

Avoid planting anything underneath deciduous trees so that you can let the leaves remain where they fall. After a rain, the leaves will become matted and remain in place. In the natural world, fallen leaves become natural fertilizer. The leaves decay, and numerous organisms feed upon them, making their nutrients available to the tree from which they fell. Nature constantly recycles matter and wastes nothing. If you must rake up leaves, add them to a compost pile.

Leaves on the ground are called leaf "litter," and most people probably view discarded leaves as being akin to trash—something that makes an area messy and unsightly. But leaf litter performs valuable services for trees and wildlife. As mulch, it maintains soil moisture and moderates soil temperature for the benefit of tree roots.

The layer of leaves also serves as shelter for numerous kinds of organisms. Leaf litter offers small animals some protection from predators, although predators do search for meals by scratching or sniffing around in it. Many kinds of treefrogs hibernate underneath leaves on the ground, as do many kinds of caterpillars in various stages of develop-

The sensible action to take if you grow a tree such as this Japanese Maple in a lawn is to allow its leaves to remain underneath it after they fall. The dried leaves will be useful as natural mulch, a refuge for wildlife, and a feeding site for animals searching among the leaves.

ment. For example, Hackberry Emperor caterpillars feed upon the leaves of Common Hackberry trees during the summer and overwinter as partially grown larvae that fall to the ground with the leaves. If you rake up all of the leaves underneath your hackberry tree and burn or compost them, you destroy all of the caterpillars as well. By killing the butterfly larvae, you deny yourself the privilege of seeing lovely Hackberry Emperors the following summer.

Many birds and small mammals are dependent upon leaf litter for food to help them make it through the winter. Sparrows, cardinals, and wrens poke among the leaves trying to find those overwintering caterpillars and pupae and other kinds of insects, and foxes would love to make a meal of semifrozen treefrogs. (Treefrogs are able to tolerate ice crystals within their bodies—something that would kill most other animals.)

Therefore, when you try to grow grass (or anything else) underneath trees, you not only make more work for yourself but also prevent many kinds of wildlife from living in your vicinity. Instead of viewing leaves on the ground as litter, think of them as an important resource for wildlife and as free mulch for your trees and shrubs. If you have evergreen trees, allow them to retain their natural shape (do not cut off the lowermost branches). Evergreen trees normally have little space between their lowest branches and the ground; therefore, you will not be tempted to plant grass under them. As with deciduous trees, allow dried fallen needles to remain as a mulch layer at the bottom of evergreens.

Too Much Mulch

Several years ago, a curious phenomenon took hold. People began to surround their trees with huge mounds of mulch that were flattened at the top, resembling miniature volcanoes. Volcano mulching has become a common sight, but this practice is very bad for trees. Indeed, numerous trees are going to be damaged, and many will die from this excess mulch.

If you apply too much mulch around a large established tree that has lived for decades with very little mulch, you may suffocate the tree's roots. Roots need access to air, just as all living things do. If you cover them with a heavy "blanket" that retains a lot of moisture, airflow will be impeded. Air molecules cannot penetrate into soil spaces that are filled with water molecules.

Death from root suffocation is a gradual process that may take several years, but the signs will be evident. Leaf yellowing in late spring results from a weakening root system that is unable to absorb enough nutrients. Plant vigor declines, as evidenced by leaves that do not reach their full size at maturity. Smaller leaves mean that less photosynthesis can take place, so the tree's rate of growth slows. With each passing year, the tree becomes weaker and weaker until it finally dies.

Such a sickly tree will be a magnet for insects, birds, and other animals, which will probably be blamed for its demise. Rodents might take advantage of the thick mulch by tunneling underneath to feed on the tree bark out of sight, in relative safety. Slugs and snails will appear to feed on the wet, decaying mulch. Disease microorganisms will thrive in

In years to come, many beloved plants are likely to succumb to damage or disease as a result of "volcano mulching," a practice that has spread through the country without resistance from nurserymen, who are supposed to know better.

the thick mulch because it rarely dries out. Yet the responsibility for the loss of an overmulched tree rests squarely on the owner's shoulders.

Gardeners are often told to mulch their plants to help retain soil moisture, so to an uninformed person, it might seem logical to heavily mulch trees during times of scarce rainfall. Indeed, one spring I received a government publication called "A Special Report to Citizens" with my property tax bill. This report recommended that residents "use abundant mulch around trees and shrubs and in plant beds to shade and hold moisture in the soil." This was horrendous advice, made all the more so because it seemed to be coming from a reputable source.

The most basic gardening rule is to always take your gardening cues from the natural world. It will never steer you wrong. If you look in woods or forestland in your area that is left to function on its own, I can guarantee that you will not find trees with thick mounds of mulch around them.

In addition to applying mulch too thickly, people sometimes pile it high right against the stems of plants. This will cause herbaceous plants (those that do not form tough, woody stems) to rot. Also, certain kinds of trees and shrubs will send out roots into the mulch, making them susceptible to drought and freeze damage because the aboveground roots are more exposed than those underground.

If you have an excessive amount of mulch around your plants, remove some of it. If the trees or shrubs have not been too seriously weakened, they may recover. If you wish to apply fresh mulch to an already mulched plant, you may have to remove some (put it on your compost pile) before adding more. You should never have more than two to three inches of mulch around a plant, and the mulch should never touch the stem; keep it several inches away.

As an organic material, mulch should begin to decay almost immediately with the help of microorganisms and to be "processed" by slugs, sow bugs, and other creatures. Do not be concerned if you see these animals in the mulch; they are working for you. They will create a nutrient-rich soil that will help your plants grow well.

Chapter 4

Feeding and
Sheltering Wildlife

Much misinformation—in books, newspaper and magazine columns, and nature club newsletters—is given to folks who want to provide food and nesting sites for wildlife. At the very least, these misguided suggestions can prevent people from enjoying wildlife because the animals disregard their efforts. At the most, poor advice can cause actual harm to wildlife.

The recommendations in this chapter are the result of many years of personal experience and observations. By heeding what I am about to share with you, you will save yourself much time, effort, and money, and you will be able to begin enjoying the company of local wildlife almost immediately.

Feeding Birds

Many kinds of animals want to partake of the food we call "birdseed." Thus, even though your plan is to feed birds, you will actually be feeding many other animals as well. This is not necessarily a bad thing; it all depends on how you go about it. If you cannot accept that wildlife will take advantage of the food you provide, you will find yourself in a frustrating battle to exclude many of the creatures around you. In order to take pleasure in feeding the birds and the other animals that visit, simply take heed of the following pointers.

Limit the amount of seed you put out each day. If you place seeds directly on the ground, put out only the amount that will be eaten by the end of the day. Even if you prefer not to throw seeds directly on the ground, whole or partially eaten seeds will inevitably find their way there, dropped by birds perched on a feeder.

During the day, many species of birds will pick up seeds on the ground (such as towhees, which prefer to poke through plant debris for their food), as will other kinds of animals, such as squirrels and ants. At night, when seed-eating birds and diurnal mammals (those that are active during the day) are sleeping, nocturnal mammals (those active at night), such as rabbits, raccoons, mice, and foxes, may come around to scavenge whatever seeds are available beneath the feeder. Turkeys might visit at dawn, and deer could show up at any time. Therefore, it is impossible to feed only the feathered creatures you probably had in mind when you provided birdseed. But do not be discouraged. Instead, welcome these other critters in your yard. They are all fulfilling a function.

However, you do not want to encourage too many animals to stay too long, because that can lead to problems. If you avoid leaving an abundance of seed on the ground, animals that stop by will find just a few seeds and will stay only briefly. They will have to move on to look for more food elsewhere and thus should not present a problem.

Do not try to make pets out of wild mammals. It is fine to feed birds, because this does not cause them to change their behavior toward humans. Birds will continue to fly away whenever a person comes near.

If you put out birdseed, you should expect mammals, such as this Common Raccoon, to try to also take advantage of your generosity.

Wild mammals, however, that come to associate humans with food can be very dangerous to both people and themselves. Never hand-feed them. You risk being bitten, and you are putting the animals at risk as well. Such animals may become beggars, approaching humans for hand-outs, because to a wild animal, all humans are the same. Once an animal has received food from one person, it may well approach other people for food. And when a wild animal approaches for no apparent reason, people are justifiably frightened, no matter what kind of animal it is. Thus, a person who encounters a seemingly unafraid animal might kill the animal—or report it to law enforcement officials, who may believe it to be rabid, and which could certainly doom it to an early and perhaps totally unnecessary demise.

Does this mean that you should not make *any* food available to wild mammals? No, it does not. The point is that the mammals should not get the idea that you are putting food out especially for them. Do *not* try to befriend them by throwing out food when they are within sight, and do not sweet-talk them as you would a pet.

Animal-Proof Bird Feeders

Mammals can smell the seeds in a hanging feeder or tray and will try to climb up to get to them. But if your feeder is on a pole with an effective baffle (not all baffles work as advertised), it will be easier to deal with these animals. (Bears, however, require special arrangements; see chapter 9.)

Numerous suppliers sell baffles in addition to poles. Baffles are often hemispherical (umbrella shaped) and made of plastic. Those constructed of very thick plastic are more durable and less easily broken than those made of thin plastic and are worth the extra expense. Some people make their own baffles using various materials, such as PVC pipe, duct pipe, or sheet metal. Some of these work quite well.

My hemispherical plastic baffles worked well for about a decade until a large raccoon figured out how to get around them. I really had to do something about this situation, because this raccoon not only ate all the seeds; it also tore my feeders apart to get to them. Luckily, I found a "Raccoon Guard" in a specialty catalog. This baffle is a heavy-duty, painted metal cylinder that is twenty-eight inches long and seven and a half inches wide. It is expensive, but it works. The Raccoon Guard also keeps the squirrels at bay and is the most effective baffle I have found. And because it is made of thick metal, it has lasted much longer (going on ten years) than plastic baffles, which are easily broken over time because of sun damage.

You cannot trust everything you are told about bird feeders. This Gray Squirrel is inside a supposedly squirrel-proof feeder.

Squirrels are probably the birds' number-one competitor for seeds, and many feeders will claim to be squirrel-proof. Most, however, are not. Some feeders have a wire barrier that resembles a cage. Often the space between the cage and the feeder inside it allows a squirrel to poke its face or its paw through the cage to reach the seed. Or the holes in some cages are too big, allowing a small squirrel to squeeze through.

Some feeders have a spring-loaded landing that closes the seed-dispenser opening when a mammal puts its weight on it. This kind of a feeder can usually be placed on a pole or hung from a hook. I have had two problems with these feeders. First, when there is a hard rain, the seeds inside get soaked because the seal is not tight enough. Therefore, I consider this to be a "fair-weather" feeder that should be emptied before a storm. Second, the feeder lid is held in place by a metal clip. I had at least one squirrel that was able to manipulate the clip and lift the lid enough to get inside and eat to its heart's content!

My advice is to ignore the supposedly squirrel-proof feeders, which may cost more than other feeders. Simply place any kind of feeder on a baffled pole, and you should be able to keep squirrels out. The top of your baffle should be at least six feet above ground level, because a Gray Squirrel can leap five vertical feet. You must also place your pole more than eight feet from plants or structures to keep it beyond a squirrel's horizontal range.

Never apply a lubricant (such as the Crisco shortening suggested in some books) to your feeder pole, no matter how safe it might seem. Sticky, greasy substances can harm wildlife in many ways. For example, raccoons may have trouble grasping food. Also, matted fur does not provide insulation against the cold in winter.

If you have a feeder hanging by a wire from a tree limb, where squirrels or other animals can approach from above, you can place a wide piece of thin sheet metal above it. The sheet metal will not support the animal's weight, dropping it to the ground. Simply make a small hole in the center of the sheet metal and slide it down over the wire until it rests on the feeder. Birds may be wary of flying under the sheet metal at first, but they will soon venture in.

Please do not buy the type of feeder that delivers an electric shock to squirrels. It is unnecessary to harm them, as there are better alternatives. One way to deter squirrels is to try to make the food you put out less attractive to them. For example, you might switch from sunflower to saf-flower seeds. However, these seeds may also be less popular with the songbirds you are trying to attract.

Many years ago, red pepper was touted as a good way to keep squir-rels from eating your birdseed. Supposedly, birds are not sensitive to capsaicin, the ingredient in hot peppers that causes the burning sensa-tion. Therefore, birds would not be averse to eating pepper-coated seeds, whereas squirrels would leave the seeds alone.

However, I consider this to be a cruel method to deter squirrels. I also worry that the pepper might get into the eyes of either birds or squirrels, causing quite an irritation. Anyway, adding red pepper may not work. Someone I know tried adding red pepper to his sunflower seeds but found that the squirrels continued to eat them.

My husband came up with a novel idea for feeding birds on our deck, where it is impossible to place a pole out of reach of jumping squir-rels. He took some wire fencing with one-inch by two-inch openings and cut off a section ten feet long and one foot wide. He formed the fencing

The author's husband created a "cage" feeder that truly is squirrel-proof.

into a circular "cage"—with a diameter large enough to prevent squirrels from reaching the central area inside—and tied the ends together. Then he bent apart every other opening around the perimeter to allow birds as large as an immature cardinal to enter. You may have to adjust the openings to get them just right, but once you do, you will have a wonderful feeder that is inexpensive and can be placed anywhere. To complete the cage, you need a piece of plywood that is big enough to lay over the top to keep squirrels from entering. The plywood cover also keeps the seeds dry and allows birds to feed in comfort on rainy or snowy days.

Birds will need some time to figure out how to enter the cage through the enlarged openings and then find their way back out. In fact, birds may panic when they cannot immediately locate an escape hole. Thus, it is important to create openings on all levels of the curved cage. This period of adjustment is painful to watch. I almost went outside several times to release a panicked bird by lifting the plywood cover up, but the bird always found its way out before I got to the cage. It only took a few weeks for the birds to figure out the system.

Thanks to my husband's ingenuity, we are now able to enjoy watching our feathered companions eating on the deck while we eat our own meals inside.

Birdseed Basics

Many kinds of birdseed are sold, but they are not all equally attractive to songbirds. Red millet, wheat, canary seed, buckwheat, and oats are often found in seed mixtures. These grains are not particularly attractive to birds, so you are wasting your money when you buy such mixes.

Unfortunately, most people purchase seed mixtures and place them into the typical bird feeder that has perches at the feeding holes. But birds that do not mind landing on small perches to feed are typically not interested in most of the seeds in a seed mixture. Consequently, few birds will make use of such feeders. Thus, it is much better for the birds and for you to buy individual bags of the kinds of seeds preferred by the birds in your area (birds in different regions of the country vary a bit in their seed preferences). Individually packaged seed allows you to place the right kind of seed into the right kind of feeder.

Two kinds of seeds should serve as the basis of a bird-feeding program anywhere in the United States: sunflower and white (not red) proso millet. These two seeds should be offered separately: sunflower in tubular feeders or any feeders with perches, and white millet in tray feeders that accommodate ground-feeding bird species. Chickadees, titmice, nuthatches, and finches frequent sunflower-filled feeders with perches.

Towhees, buntings, sparrows, and doves readily come to tray feeders containing white millet.

There are two varieties of sunflower seeds: black oil and striped. Black oil is smaller and thus is often easier for some birds to eat. Its high oil content provides lots of energy. Striped sunflower seed is larger and has less oil content. Birds with beaks capable of cracking the shell readily eat this seed, but it is not nearly as popular as black oil. There are also "blended" sunflower seed mixtures that consist of both kinds of sunflower seeds, and if the price is right, you might want to buy such a mix. Otherwise, I recommend black oil as the superior seed.

Some species of birds (such as Carolina Wrens) do not have beaks capable of breaking open sunflower seed shells. These birds require sunflower seeds that are already cracked (exposing the kernel inside) or hulled (these shell-less seeds are referred to as sunflower chips, pieces, or hearts). Hulled sunflower seeds are attractive to virtually all species of seed-eating birds, even those that eat white millet (Brown-headed Cowbirds are unusual, in that they seem to prefer millet). However, hulled seeds are much more expensive per pound, because you are paying for the labor involved in removing the shells. On the plus side, you are buying only edible food that virtually any bird might eat.

One winter in central Virginia, we had a severe cold spell following a big snowstorm. For almost two weeks, all the plants were covered in ice, which meant that fruit-eating birds had great difficulty getting anything to eat. During this frigid period, a Hermit Thrush (an insect- and fruit-eating bird) showed up on my deck every day and stayed for hours, drawn by the hulled sunflower seeds that I put out daily. I have no doubt that my expensive hulled sunflower seeds helped save the life of that bird (otherwise, the thrush would not have been such a regular visitor).

Hulled sunflower seeds may also assist birds that nest early. If temperatures plummet in the spring, causing insects to be inactive, the adults can feed sunflower bits to their chicks. I have watched Carolina Wrens taking sunflower bits to their nestlings on chilly March days when insects were not active. Again, I have no doubt that those sunflower pieces helped the chicks survive a period of insect scarcity.

I highly recommend using hulled sunflower seeds for feeding areas where you do not want shell litter under the feeder, such as in a lawn, where a thick layer of shells may kill the grass. Another problem with feeding sunflower seeds in the shell is that you will probably end up with numerous sunflower seedlings when spring arrives. Dropped seeds are viable and will germinate. If you want to avoid having to pull out

Shelled sunflower pieces can be eaten by virtually any kind of bird. If cold weather hits, Carolina Wrens that nest early in the season may find insect pickings slim and have trouble gathering enough food for their nestlings. The availability of sunflower pieces could save the day!

unwanted sunflower plants, it may be worthwhile to feed only hulled sunflower seeds. Uneaten white millet and milo seeds that fall to the ground can also germinate, so you might want to be careful about where you serve these seeds as well. For all these reasons, I always have hulled sunflower seeds in at least one feeder. To save money, I feed whole, unhulled sunflower seeds in feeders where it does not matter if shells pile up or seedlings sprout.

If you want to provide your birds with a bit of variety, there are other kinds of seeds to consider. Niger seed (sometimes spelled "nyjer"), imported from Nigeria, is very enticing to American Goldfinches, Mourning Doves, and Pine Siskins. Niger is rather expensive, however, so you might want to think of it as a rare treat that you do not offer on a regular basis. Finches will come for sunflower seeds and doves for white millet just as readily. Part of the reason for its high cost is that the seeds are sterilized, so you do not have to worry about niger seedlings under your feeder.

Some feeders are specially made to dispense niger seed. They have tiny holes so that the very thin niger seeds do not come pouring out. I have found, however, that any tube feeder will work. What looks like fallen seeds are, upon closer inspection, simply the discarded shells. A bird does not swallow the entire seed but cracks it open to eat the kernel or meat inside.

Corn is an inexpensive grain that is quite attractive to numerous species of birds and mammals. Coarse cracked corn—the broken kernels that farmers feed to their poultry—is probably the easiest for wild birds to eat. Whole corn can be difficult to break open with small beaks, and fine cracked corn can be a mess if it gets wet. Cardinals, sparrows, doves, and towhees readily eat corn that is placed either on the ground or in tray feeders.

Milo is another seed that is often found in seed mixtures. Mourning Doves eat it readily, especially those in the western United States. Milo that falls on the ground is eagerly eaten by rabbits as well.

Whole peanuts in the shell can be offered to birds in special feeders that look like little round cages. Peanut bits and pieces can be placed in hopper feeders. Tufted Titmice, Blue Jays, and Red-bellied Woodpeckers come readily to peanuts.

Although I know many people who delight in feeding peanuts to their birds, I prefer to put out peanut butter. I find it easier to store (it takes up less space and stays fresh longer), and I believe that it is more readily eaten by a larger variety of birds. I enjoy watching Tufted Titmice, Carolina Wrens, Northern Cardinals, Dark-eyed Juncos, Brown Creepers, White-breasted Nuthatches, Blue Jays, Yellow-bellied Sapsuckers, chickadees, and sparrows eating peanut butter. And there is nothing better for bringing woodpeckers into view.

For birds that can cling to a vertical surface, you can simply smear the peanut butter on dead trees or pinecones. To make it easier for birds that have trouble clinging (for example, cardinals, sparrows, and juncos), you can place the peanut butter on a flat surface, such as a tray or a stump with a level top.

Pure peanut butter can be served, but I make a peanut butter mixture. I melt two cups of shortening and stir in an eighteen-ounce jar of inexpensive peanut butter (creamy or chunky) until it is soupy and well mixed. I stiffen up the mixture for spreadability by adding about five cups of flour, cornmeal, or a mix of both. The final quantity of dry ingredients depends on the brand of peanut butter, with some being oilier than others and requiring more flour or cornmeal.

As you add the dry ingredients and the mixture cools, you will reach a point at which the mixture is not too sticky and not too crumbly. Scoop it into containers and store them in the freezer. When you want to put some peanut butter out for the birds, let the container come to room temperature before trying to remove the peanut butter.

Other kinds of animals, such as squirrels and raccoons, enjoy peanut butter too. To keep them from eating all of it, you can make a peanut butter stick from a tree branch. Hollow out one-inch-diameter holes partway into the branch, add a loop of wire at the top, and hang the peanut butter stick on a baffled pole out of reach of the mammals. You can also place the peanut butter mix in a suet basket. These wire baskets can be found at any store that sells bird-feeding supplies.

Additionally, I have drilled holes in snags (standing dead trees) and filled them with peanut butter. These trees are magnets for woodpeckers. In the summer, the adults bring their begging fledglings and feed them peanut butter at the snag. Later, when the fledglings have become inde-pendent, they can be seen feeding themselves at the snag. Red-bellied, Downy, Hairy, and even Pileated Woodpeckers have all visited my peanut butter snags with their beg-ging young in tow.

When the squirrels discovered this source of peanut butter, they rapidly depleted my supply during the day, and raccoons took their place at night. To remedy this situa-tion, I placed one-quarter-inch hard-ware cloth (sold at most hardware stores) over the holes. The birds can still get the peanut butter through the openings in the screen, but the squirrels and raccoons cannot.

If you do not have any natural snags, you might be able to create artificial ones, as I did. Although I had plenty of snags on my property, I wanted some near my bay window so that I could take photos of the birds that came in to feed. A neigh-bor brought me some locust logs, which I "planted" vertically in my front yard. (Two of them were six feet long, and the third was twelve feet long.) Locust wood is slow to decay, so it makes for great artificial snags. I used a posthole digger to plant my three pieces, with about one-third of each below ground level. I also stomped in the dirt around them to add stability.

Woodpeckers absolutely love peanut butter and will visit your yard all win-ter for it. In the East, if you can con-tinue to put it out until the end of June, you may get to see parent woodpeckers feeding their young.

Since putting in my snags, I have learned a lot about the different species of woodpeckers. I know when they reproduce, based on when they arrive with their young begging for food. I also discovered that immature male Red-bellied, Downy, and Hairy Woodpeckers have different plumages from their parents and that these young woodpeckers have distinctive calls. It has been fascinating. I learned more about woodpeckers in the first year I had peanut butter snags near my house than in the previous thirty years I had been feeding birds.

The Bird-Feeding Controversy

Bird feeding is a controversial topic. Some ornithologists are concerned about the spread of disease at crowded feeders. Other researchers believe that hawks are better able to prey upon birds bunched together in feeding areas. Some scientists worry that feeders help nonnative species, and others believe that there is simply no need to feed birds.

A study that was completed more than two decades ago may have ignited this controversy. A graduate student observing Black-capped Chickadees in Wisconsin concluded that "bird feeding has less impact on birds than is popularly assumed" and that it was unnecessary to feed birds to help them survive. However, the study was flawed. It took place in a remote rural location where no feeders were present. Birds found in such an area—a habitat minimally altered by humans—should be expected to survive on a natural diet, because birds can live only where all the conditions for their survival are met. Thus, it is not appropriate to apply the results of this particular study to urban and suburban areas, where the habitat is very much altered by humans and where there is not much natural food available for birds, especially during the winter and early spring—thanks to prevalent gardening practices.

Year after year, people are told by the horticultural industry that they must clean up their plants in autumn to avoid providing overwintering sites for insects. As a result of this yearly sanitation of the natural world, both seeds and insects are destroyed that could have provided essential foods for wildlife. Additionally, people are often told that it is fine to suddenly stop feeding birds (for example, if they are going away on vacation), but I find this advice to be questionable. Perhaps you could ask a friend or neighbor to fill your feeders while you are gone, along with watering your houseplants or feeding your fish. As long as people continue to heed misguided horticultural advice, very little natural food will be available for birds and other creatures.

Another strong criticism of bird feeding is the increased probability of spreading diseases among birds because of the crowded conditions.

However, the chance of spreading disease can be lessened. Be sure to keep your feeder clean, promptly removing fecal droppings and decaying food. Disinfect your feeder by soaking it for two to three minutes in a mixture of one part bleach and nine parts warm water. Let the feeder dry completely before refilling it. Even if you are conscientious about maintaining your feeders in tip-top form, you may still see a sick bird, but you should not feel guilty. In the real world, animals become ill and die.

To avoid making your birds "sitting ducks" for hawks, be sure to provide shelter—in the form of shrubs, trees, or brush piles—no closer than nine feet from your feeders.

Another potential danger when feeding birds is that they might fly into windows. Hawk decals are helpful, although they would work better if they were white instead of black; even better would be a shiny, reflective, bright-colored material. Hawk decals do not eliminate collisions, but they often slow birds down enough so that they are only stunned instead of killed. White blinds that are kept closed or mostly closed during the day are also extremely effective. As with the hawk decals, darker-colored blinds tend to disappear behind the glass. Window screens can help prevent collisions because they do not reflect the sky and trees as glass windows do. Also, if a bird does hit a screen, it is likely to just bounce off and not be severely injured.

The Yellow-billed Cuckoo is a bird of the forest, and you would not expect it to fly under a porch roof and into a window. Yet that is exactly what this one did.

However, birds do not necessarily hit windows because they are at your feeders. I have had Red-eyed Vireos and even a Yellow-billed Cuckoo—both birds of the woods that eat insects and are rather secretive—hit my porch windows that are under cover of a roof. Unless you live in a house devoid of windows, bird collisions are, unfortunately, bound to happen.

You need not feel guilty about feeding birds, so long as you regard it as a serious responsibility. And if you garden naturally—letting flowers go to seed and remain standing throughout the winter—birds and many other species of wildlife will find it easier to survive.

Providing Shelter

Many birds and mammals nest or eat their meals inside natural cavities or excavated cavities of their own making in rotted-out sections of trees. Invertebrates, such as insects and spiders, also take advantage of cavities or the shelter offered by the loose bark of a dead tree to survive the cold months of winter. Thus, dead trees are a crucial component of the natural environment.

Unfortunately, because dead trees can eventually pose a hazard to humans, they are rare in the home landscape. If you cannot leave such trees standing because of safety concerns, you can provide artificial shelter and nesting sites by putting up bird boxes—or, more accurately, wildlife boxes, because they will probably be used by other animals as well. Bat boxes and toad shelters are additional accommodations that will help make your yard a nature wonderland.

Wildlife Boxes

Bluebirds, chickadees, titmice, squirrels, and even flying squirrels and screech-owls may take up residence in a box outside your house if you provide them with a suitable place in an appropriate habitat. If you observe these animals in your area (or you hear screech-owls at night), your chances of enticing them to an artificial cavity are quite good.

Winter is a great time to think about making or buying birdhouses and putting them up. The cold weather may entice you to stay indoors to do woodworking, and when you are ready to put the boxes outside, the cold weather creates safer conditions for doing so. The bees and wasps that may be nesting in trees and flying around your house during the warmer months are not likely to be encountered. For the same reason, winter is also a good time to clean out existing boxes.

It is a good idea to buy boxes from a reputable source (nature organizations, stores that specialize in nature products) or to make them yourself by consulting a good how-to book. Each species of bird prefers a particular cavity size in which to nest. Thus, it is very important that you make or buy a birdhouse that meets the requirements of the species you are trying to help. You must take into account the interior dimensions of the birdhouse, the entrance hole size, and the distance between the hole and the floor of the house. When placing the boxes on trees, you need to put them at the proper height above the ground. You can find such information in books or magazines or obtain it from your state wildlife agency or nature organizations. However, some of the "common knowledge" about the construction and placement of boxes is actually misguided. Additionally, some sources may leave out critical information that can result in the death of nestlings. I address these deficiencies here, along with other important points, based on my decades of experience using wildlife boxes in my own yard.

Never buy or make bird or bat houses out of treated wood. According to the American Wood Preservers Institute, pressure-treated wood is resistant to decay and insects because it has been treated with powerful pesticides. In the past, inorganic arsenic, creosote, or pentachlorophenol was employed, but more recently, alkaline copper quaternary (ACQ) and copper azole (CA) have been used. All these chemicals are dangerous if ingested or absorbed through the skin. Therefore, pressure-treated wood should *never* be employed for bird or bat houses. The animals may peck at or gnaw on the wood and may be in direct contact with it for hours at a time over the course of many days. If you are concerned about longevity, houses should be built of cedar, which resists decay naturally.

Never apply paint or other coatings to the inside surfaces of a wildlife box. The fumes can be deadly to wildlife (and people) when inhaled. However, it may be a good idea to apply paint or wood preservative to the outside surfaces to help make the wood last longer. If you do this, be sure to leave the box outside in the sun for a few days, where it can completely air out and dry, before you put it up for use by wildlife. Also, leave a two- to three-inch ring of untreated wood around the outside of the entrance hole to provide a rough surface for birds landing there; this is easier for them to grasp.

Be certain to rough up the inside surface between the entrance hole and the floor of the box. Young birds may have difficulty climbing up to the opening when the time comes for them to leave, and a rough surface enhances a nestling's ability to grip the wood. Birds with especially weak feet, such as Tree Swallows, can die in smooth-sided boxes because they are unable to get out.

I have found that screech-owls prefer a larger entrance than the three-inch hole generally recommended in books. If you construct your own screech-owl box, make the entrance hole four to four and a half inches in diameter. Screech-owls sometimes like to perch on the rim of the entrance hole when roosting during the winter or when the owlets are beginning to take up more space inside the box. (Screech-owl parents remain inside the box with their young during the day until it becomes too cramped. Then the male starts roosting outside on a nearby tree, followed by the adult female several days later.) When the entrance hole is

Eastern Screech-Owls like to perch on the rim of a box opening during the day, especially if it is cold and the box is in the sun. Conventional wisdom states that the opening should be only three inches in diameter, but the author highly recommends that it be four to four and a half inches in diameter.

large enough, the owlets will also perch on the rim when they are within a few days of fledging. That is a real treat to witness!

Screws are better than nails in box construction. They do not become unattached as easily. If you must buy a box made with nails, you can replace the nails with screws or add some screws. Predrilling a hole before putting in a screw minimizes the chance of the wood splitting.

It is especially important to use screws to attach boxes to trees. As a tree grows, it produces a lot of force on the attachment points. A box nailed to a tree can easily be dislodged, whereas a box screwed to a tree resists the outward forces because of the screw's threading. Be sure to check the stability of the box before every nesting season; eventually, the box will loosen. Use only rust-resistant galvanized screws for structures placed outside.

Never buy or make a box with the opening panel at the bottom of the structure. You will not be able to tell whether anyone is still home before you open the box and start cleaning out the contents, which could be disastrous. It is better for the opening panel to be located on the side or at the front of the box and to swing out and away from the box rather than opening into the box. The latter makes it difficult for you to peer into the box and makes it more difficult for an animal to quickly exit the box. Finally, the opening panel should be easy to open without the use of tools, preferably by means of a hand-operated latch. The more convenient it is to get inside the box, the easier it will be for you to maintain it.

If you put out boxes of many different sizes for many different kinds of birds, disregard the advice to place boxes for different species at various heights. If you have a lot of houses, as I do, it gets tiresome to constantly adjust the height of the ladder in order to reach into the boxes for their annual cleaning. It is also unnecessary. Small boxes (those with inside dimensions of about four inches by four inches and six to eight inches high) can simply be placed five to six feet above the ground. Bigger boxes (those with inside dimensions of at least six inches by six inches and ten or more inches high) can be placed at about twelve to fifteen feet. As long as your boxes are sited where they will accommodate the temperature needs of the intended wildlife, these heights should be fine.

If no animal has made use of a box within three years, try to figure out what could be wrong and correct it. Sometimes a box may be receiving too much sunshine, making it too hot during nesting time. (Note that bats are an exception; they prefer hot areas, so bat boxes should be placed high on a tree facing south.) Or the box may be located too deep in the woods or not deep enough. To attract a nester to your box, you need to know what conditions must be met. Only then will you be able to determine the correct spot for the box.

Last but not least, do not harass the animals using your nest boxes. Many nature enthusiasts "monitor" their nest boxes on a weekly basis (or more often), opening the boxes to make sure all is well or to take photographs. However, to the creatures inside the box, a human being represents a threat. Whether the creature is an adult or a baby, it has no way of knowing that you mean no harm. It must be terrifying for an animal to see a human being only inches away or to have a camera flash go off in its face. If you must satisfy your curiosity, this is best done only when the adult is away from the nest and the babies are only a few days old. If you check the box when the chicks are older, especially if they are within just a few days of fledging, you may cause them to exit the nest prematurely. Young birds that enter the world before they are ready to do so are unlikely to survive very long.

Wildlife should be watched rather than interfered with. You are supposed to be helping wildlife by creating habitat and giving it the opportunity to coexist with you. Once wildlife moves in, let nature take its course. Humans did not create the natural world, and humans are not wise enough to orchestrate how it works. So please, watch nature, but do not interfere with it. Only then will you truly learn about the natural world.

Toad Shelters

Many children like toads, perhaps because they are often characters in children's stories. Adult gardeners also like toads because these amphibians help keep down insect populations. If you want to make your yard more hospitable to these animals, try providing some toad shelters. A toad shelter is really just a hideaway where a toad can stay out of sight until nightfall without getting too hot and thus becoming susceptible to water loss.

The easiest way to provide one is to dig out a shallow trough in a shaded area, wet the soil, and cover most of the trough with a piece of lumber or a log. Both ends of the trough should be open so that the toad can escape should a predator enter from one side. It is not absolutely necessary to wet the soil in the trench, but doing so will furnish drinking water for any toads that come to visit. Toads "drink" through their skin, so during a drought, wetting the dirt is particularly helpful. Unless there is flowing or standing water in the area, it may be quite difficult for toads to get the water they need.

Toads do not drink water as other animals do; they absorb it through their skin. This American Toad backed its way into a pot of impatiens cuttings that were in wet soil to encourage root development.

Another way to provide a toad shelter is to use a ten- to twelve-inch-diameter clay flowerpot turned upside down. Break off a small piece of the rim on two opposite sides for entranceways by gently tapping the edge with a hammer. (You must make two holes so that the toad can escape out of one if a predator comes through the other.) It is okay if the edges are jagged, so long as the height and width of each hole is just big enough—about two to three inches— for a toad to fit through. Find a shady part of your garden or yard, wet the soil, and lay the new toad shelter down over the damp soil.

Once a toad finds the shelter, it will probably make use of it almost daily. You may peek under the toad shelter occasionally to see if it is being used, but please do not look too often. A toad needs its privacy!

Paving the Way for Butterflies

You may have noticed that butterflies gather at damp spots or puddles along dirt roads or anywhere rainwater remains on the ground before evaporating. The minerals concentrated in these areas make it easier for butterflies to obtain the additional nutrients they need for mating.

Almost all of the butterflies that "puddle" are males. A male needs salt, amino acids, and other nutrients to pass along with his sperm (in a package called a spermatophore) when he mates with a female. The additional nutrients probably help the female to produce eggs. Because there is very little salt in plants (the main food source of caterpillars and butterflies), the adults need to supplement their diets by obtaining salt from other sources. Besides damp soil, these insects also visit carrion. I once saw a bright yellow Eastern Tiger Swallowtail on a dead raccoon. The beauty of the butterfly seemed totally out of place on the rotting carcass. Butterflies (and moths) also land on scat (animal fecal droppings) and urination sites that contain salt and other nutrients.

But if you have a concrete carport or sidewalk or decorative concrete lawn ornaments in your yard, you may spot these insects puddling there as well. Apparently, they are able to obtain nutrients from concrete, which is made by mixing cement, sand, and gravel together with water. Cement is composed of alumina, silica, lime, iron oxide, and magnesium oxide, which are burned together in a kiln and finely pulverized. Therefore, cement is probably the chief source of minerals for a butterfly stroking a concrete surface with its proboscis. The insect exudes saliva through its proboscis down to the concrete and then sucks it back up again, apparently picking up minute particles of concrete in the process.

The butterflies that visit my concrete carport floor and concrete birdbath pedestal look very beautiful and fresh, as if they have just emerged from their chrysalids. So— as strange as it may seem—you might want to add some concrete to your wildlife habitat!

A Red Admiral butterfly uses its proboscis to suck minerals from a carport floor.

1. **Minimize rototilling.** If you create a garden on hard subsoil that has very little organic matter in it, you will probably need to employ a rototiller to break up the earth. You will also need to add organic matter to enrich the soil and make it friable. After several years, many earthworms and millipedes will have taken up residence to feed upon and incorporate bits of plant material into the soil. And other organisms, such as centipedes and salamanders, will have moved in to feed upon the plant eaters to keep their numbers in check.

   At this point, using a rototiller is unnecessary; it will maim or kill the creatures that are working so hard for you. It is better to work the garden by hand. Loosen up one small area at a time to prepare it for planting seeds, and make individual holes for transplants (a bulb planter works great). Your wildlife will thank you for your consideration by keeping the garden functioning just as it should be!

People often overlook the wildlife habitat at and below ground level. Yet the animals that reside here, such as these Redback Salamanders, are intensely helpful to the proper functioning of your garden.

2. **Be very careful when pruning or otherwise working in your yard.** When you encourage wildlife to share your property, it is quite likely that you will uncover nesting or resting animals when you do yard work. Always keep your eyes open so that you do not inadvertently harm or disturb any creatures. Yard work can usually be delayed to accommodate your wildlife without harming the plants you wanted to work on.

You never know what you might find when working with your plants. This large trapdoor spider, a tarantula relative, was found in the author's garden when a blueberry bush was being relocated.

3. **Do not leave your lights on—inside or outside—unless absolutely necessary.** Lights attract insects that should be feeding or mating. Many kinds of insects are disappearing, in part due to the prevalence of man-made night lighting.

4. **Never use a bug zapper.** These electrical devices are nonselective, attracting and killing numerous kinds of insects unnecessarily.

5. **Always use *white sugar* to prepare hummingbird food.** Never use honey, brown sugar, or artificial sweeteners (including Splenda). A mixture made with white sugar closely resembles the naturally occurring nectar in flowers. Mixtures made with the other ingredi-

ents can kill hummingbirds. Boil one cup of water and one cup of sugar until the sugar is thoroughly dissolved. Then add three more cups of cold water so that the final mixture is four parts water to one part sugar. Do not increase this concentration of sugar, or the mixture will grow mold more quickly. Fill your feeder, and store the leftover sugar solution in the refrigerator. Clean your feeder every two to three days to prevent the growth of mold that can kill hummers.

6. **Leave spiderwebs alone.** A spiderweb is a work of art that is much more attractive than a sticky trap for reducing insect populations. Using pesticides to kill insects removes links from the food chain. A spider that eats insects becomes food for a bird, which might serve as food for a snake, which could be caught by a hawk.

It does not matter what kind of hummingbird feeder you use as long as it is easy to clean. Remember that anything other than white sugar may kill hummingbirds

7. **Allow mushrooms to grow in your lawn or mulch.** Mushrooms enrich the soil and keep predator-prey relationships working to your benefit. They tell you that there is dead plant or animal matter in the environment that needs to be broken down and recycled. They also serve as food for numerous organisms, such as the larvae of the Gold-and-brown Rove Beetles, the adults of which feed upon maggots, mites, and grubs.

Chapter 5

Providing Water
for Wildlife

No matter where you live, providing a water source in your yard will bring in wildlife that you might not otherwise see. For example, many migratory birds are mostly insect eaters. Therefore, even if they nest around your house during the warmer months, you may not catch a glimpse of them because they do not usually visit feeders. However, you might be able to lure migratory species into your field of view with a birdbath or artificial pond where they can bathe or get a drink.

In arid regions of the United States, where there are few natural bodies of water, you can attract all kinds of wildlife by making water available in your location. A reliable water source is so important to wildlife that it could be called a wildlife magnet.

Numerous kinds of animals that live or lay their eggs in naturally wet locations, such as ponds or vernal pools (areas with standing water in springtime that tend to dry out later in the season), may pay a visit to an artificial pond to mate and lay eggs or to take up residence. One of my plastic ponds is only about five feet long by three feet wide, yet this small body of water has become

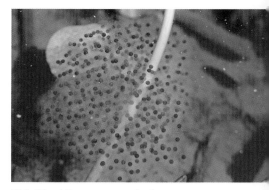

This Wood Frog egg mass in the author's little pond illustrates the usefulness of artificially created water sources for wildlife.

home to Eastern (or Red-spotted) Newts, which can often be seen swimming lazily in the water even during the coldest months of the year. Green Frogs also hang out at the pond, sitting on the surrounding rocks or floating in the water throughout the spring, summer, and fall. In the winter, they hibernate in the thin layer of muck that I allow to accumulate at the bottom of the pond, about eighteen inches beneath the surface, where the water does not freeze.

During summer, adult dragonflies and damselflies catch insects on the wing all around my house, and ultimately, these fascinating and marvelously colored creatures mate and lay their eggs in my ponds. The immature forms of these insects are aquatic and develop underwater. They are referred to as naiads (NAY-ads). Some of the dragonfly and damselfly naiads become food for larger organisms in the pond, while those that escape predators feed on numerous creatures smaller than themselves. Depending on the species of the dragonfly or damselfly, some individuals reach maturity and leave the pond by summer's

Dragonfly larvae are aquatic and are therefore often referred to as naiads. They look quite different from the adult insects that they will become.

end. Other individuals overwinter in the muck at the bottom of the pond. The following spring, after the water and air have warmed, the naiads climb up out of the water onto a plant stalk, shed their outer layer (called an exoskeleton) one last time, and eventually fly away in the adult stage that most people are familiar with.

Without a doubt, providing water is one of the best things you can do to attract wildlife.

Water Receptacles: Simple to Elaborate

The simplest way to provide water is to place a pan of it on the ground. If the pan is not too deep (one and a half to two inches is ideal), birds will use the pan not only to drink but also to bathe. Toads will hop into the pan to get the water they need to absorb through their skin.

Songbirds prefer shallow water sources because they cannot swim. They will drink from a deep pan but will not bathe in it. You should take

A birdbath must be less than two inches deep for birds to wade in and take a bath. Because these avian creatures cannot swim, they are afraid of deep water.

this into consideration when planning what kind of container to use, because bathing is critical to a bird's survival (even in the freezing temperatures of winter). Dirty feathers can get matted down, hindering a bird's ability to fly and keep warm. A bird needs clean feathers so that they can be fluffed up, trapping pockets of air within them. Trapped air provides insulation, thus helping to keep the bird's body heat from escaping (air is not a good conductor, so it impedes energy loss).

Although there are two artificial ponds in my yard that animals can use, I also keep a pan of fresh water on my deck floor, which is about six feet above ground level. Quite a few kinds of creatures seem to prefer to come up onto the deck to drink. One year I watched in utter fascination for several days in a row as honeybees visited that pan of water. The days were quite hot, so I believe the bees were bringing water to their hive to cool it off. For hours at a time, and at any given moment, five or six bees would be coming to the water pan as others were leaving. I wanted to know where their

Even insects need water, and they will get it at your birdbath. During several hot days, these honeybees came to the author's deck water pan. They may have been bringing the water back to their hive to cool it off.

hive was located, but I could not track the tiny creatures with my eyes. After a bee spent several moments drinking, it would fly straight up and over the top of the twenty-foot-tall Chinese Photinias (often sold as Redtips) that line my deck. Then it would zoom off, and I would lose sight of it.

Even the largest type of animal in my area—the American Black Bear—comes to that deck pan of water. It is somewhat surprising that so many of the larger critters feel safe on the deck. I surmise that they feel comfortable because the deck seems secluded due to the plants that surround it. The pan is located right outside sliding glass doors, affording me wonderful viewing and picture-taking opportunities of the many kinds of wildlife that share my home.

If you wish to serve water in a more ornate and aesthetically pleasing container, numerous birdbaths are available, from the simple and utilitarian to the ornate, at quite a range of prices. The basic form consists of a pedestal that supports a large saucer or dish. Unfortunately, many of these birdbaths are more decorative than useful; if the dish is deeper than two inches, birds will come for a drink but not for a bath.

Birdbaths may be made of concrete, plastic, or metal. Each material has its drawbacks. Concrete is heavy, which makes moving the structure difficult. It also requires cleaning once a week or more during warm weather, because algae grow easily on its surface. And concrete birdbaths cannot be used during the winter because the water may freeze within the minute surface pores, causing the birdbath to crack.

Plastic degrades more rapidly in sunlight than other materials do. Plastic is also lightweight, which makes a birdbath constructed of this material easy to tip over. However, the pedestal is usually hollow, so you can fill it with sand to weigh the base down.

Metal is probably the best material for a birdbath. It can be used year-round; it is lighter than concrete, so it is more easily moved; and it does not seem to grow algae as easily as concrete, so it does not need to be scrubbed as often.

Another consideration is whether you want a birdbath that has a design on the bath's interior surface—supposedly to make the surface less slippery for birds. However, the nooks and crannies created by a pattern can make cleaning the bath more difficult than cleaning one with a plain surface. And I have not noticed birds using my birdbaths that have plain surfaces experiencing any problems.

Birdbaths should be located in a sunny to partly shady spot with some shrubbery several feet away. The shrubbery provides nearby perches where wet birds can shake themselves off and preen. It also serves as a sanctuary for birds that need to get away from an attacking hawk. The birdbath should not be placed right next to shrubbery—the close cover allows cats to hide under the bushes and pounce upon unsuspecting bathing birds.

You should place your birdbath on a level surface. A patio of concrete, brick, or flagstones would be ideal. If you must place the birdbath on soil, be sure to smooth out the surface. Otherwise, the dish will not be level, and the water will pool to one side. (This will not bother the birds, but it may bother you to look at it.)

A birdbath in the yard should have decorative gravel piled around the base of the pedestal. Because the dish will have to be emptied and cleaned periodically, the gravel will keep soil from being washed away. First, however, place a fabric barrier (available from gardening catalogs or your local nursery) on the ground to prevent unwanted plants from coming up between the stones. Plastic is a cheaper option than fabric, but it allows the dumped water to puddle, whereas the fabric is water permeable. Puddles of standing water serve as breeding grounds for mosquitoes. Cut a piece of fabric just long enough to extend a couple of feet on either side of the birdbath. Smooth it out and spread enough gravel over it to hide the fabric. This barrier will not totally eliminate unwanted plants, but it does help to minimize your upkeep. Of course, you may decide that you like some of the plants that mysteriously appear around the birdbath.

Fresh water is as important to the health of birds and other animals as it is to humans. Therefore, try to change the water every day, especially if it is dirty. By changing the water daily or every other day, you will not have to worry about your birdbath becoming a mosquito breeding ground. Any eggs that might be laid in the water will be dumped out, killing them. Never buy an insecticide touted to kill mosquito eggs and larvae, as it will also kill other insects that might come to the water.

How often you have to scrub down the birdbath depends mostly upon algae buildup. If there is enough algae to make the bath slippery, birds may no longer bathe in it. You might consider painting a concrete birdbath with swimming-pool paint that is non-toxic to birds. The paint inhibits the growth of algae. *Never use chemicals of any kind in your birdbath water.* To rid the birdbath of algal growth, give it a periodic scouring with a weak bleach solution. Be sure to wear plastic gloves, as bleach is very harsh to the skin. If your birdbath is made of concrete or metal, use an old scrubby pad or scrubby-sided sponge that you have retired from service on your kitchen pots and pans. If your birdbath is plastic, use only a scrubby pad made for use on nonstick pans to avoid scratching the plastic. When you are done cleaning, rinse the bath with water and place it where sunshine can completely dry its surface. Then you can refill the bath with water and watch the parade of guests.

Do not think of cleaning the birdbath as a chore; think of it as taking care of the wildlife that brings you so much pleasure and so many benefits.

Ponds

For years, I felt that my landscape was incomplete. Although I loved my property, I missed the water wildlife I had observed as a child, kneeling down and peering into various creeks and streams. As an adult, I had no time to spare to go looking for water creatures; I wanted to see amphibians and fish and water insects right outside my door.

An incredible assortment of animals will move into your artificial pond. These Eastern Newts are a type of aquatic salamander.

Nowadays, it is relatively easy to do just that. Many garden centers and home improvement stores sell preformed heavy-duty polyethylene or fiberglass pond liners that are not difficult to install. The plastic liners are supposed to last about twenty years, and the more expensive fiberglass ones are supposed to last much longer. The liners come in a variety of shapes and sizes, so one is bound to suit your fancy. You can also create a pond using a thick rubber lining of forty to sixty mil instead of buying a preformed pond liner. However, this project takes a lot more effort and know-how to do correctly. No matter what kind of pond liner you use, detailed installation instructions should be available at the store where you buy the materials.

Before going to the store, however, survey your property to be sure you have a good spot for a pond. Preferably, you should be able to see it from the house. Placing your watery oasis near a window will make it easier for you to look out and watch the goings-on. The pond should also be placed where it will receive a minimum of four to six hours of sunlight a day. Your pond will require aquatic plants to function properly, and most of these plants require a good deal of sunlight.

This small pond is located near the author's bay window, where it's easy to see what's happening.

You might want to avoid areas near large trees that will shade the pond as well as drop their leaves and other debris into it. Getting some plant material into the pond is not a serious problem and is actually necessary to allow muck (decayed plant and animal matter) to form at the bottom, where frogs and other critters hibernate. However, too much decaying debris can deplete the water of oxygen. The process by which organic material breaks down is mostly aerobic, which means that it uses oxygen. Thus, it is important to limit the amount of decaying material in your pond to avoid depleting the water of the oxygen needed by the wildlife living there.

If you do have lots of big trees close to your pond, as I do, you simply have to check the pond now and then for fallen leaves and twigs. Use waterproof gloves or a net to remove the debris and put it into a big plastic container. Check the collected debris carefully—once when you first place it into the container, and again minutes later as you empty the container—for animals, and return any that you find to the pond. Then put the remaining material on a compost pile or use it as mulch around your plants.

Although you might consider it work to keep the pond surface clean of debris, the reward is a greater intimacy with the animals living underneath the water's surface. The necessity of getting close enough to remove leaves, seeds, and other plant material brings you down to where the action is and almost forces you to gaze into the water.

In the fall, many people place netting above their ponds to catch falling debris. If you decide to go this route, keep the netting strung a few inches above the water on support poles rather than weighing it down at the edges on the ground. You do not want to imprison pond residents that want to leave the water, nor do you want to ensnare snakes that may get caught in the netting. I place a metal screen of wire fencing over the middle of one of my ponds to minimize the amount of leaves I need to remove. I take it off as soon as the trees have lost most of their leaves. The openings in the fencing are two inches by four inches, which is big enough for a snake to pass through. However, both long edges of the pond are left open so that no animal actually needs to poke its head or move its body through the screen openings.

If you place fencing over your artificial pond, be sure to keep it a few inches above the water surface to allow critters to come and go easily. These Green Frogs did not mind resting at the edge of the pond underneath the fencing.

Locate your pond in a fairly level spot; the water surface should be even around the rim. Do not put the liner edge flush with the surrounding land, as this makes it easier for dirt, debris, and runoff from the yard to end up in the pond. This is especially important if you use pesticides on your lawn grass or other plants (although it is obviously preferable that you eliminate all pesticide usage). Instead, leave the edge an inch or so above the soil surface. Over time, the lip will be obscured by soil or plant material and will be less noticeable.

Many people lay rocks around the perimeter of the pond to help hide the lip. However, large animals stepping on the rocks may send them tumbling to the bottom of the pond, possibly injuring pond animals. If you decide to use rocks, try to ensure their stability.

Growing short plants around the pond will make the area feel more natural and help hide the lip. Choose plants that are not much over six inches tall so that they neither shade the pond nor obscure your view of it from inside the house.

Nonjumping animals, such as salamanders, may have trouble exiting the pond if the water level is not close to the top edge. They may not be able to climb up the vertical pond walls. Therefore, I place a long stick into each of my ponds so that animals can easily climb out. One end rests on the lip and the other end is submerged.

The pond does not have to be very big to support wildlife (three to four feet in diameter will do), but at least one section should be deep enough so that the water will not completely freeze during the winter. Preformed liners usually have a very deep area in the middle of the pond and a shallower area near the edge.

The dimensions of your pond determine how many (or, more accurately, how few) plants can be grown without overcrowding them. Plants will not grow well or stay healthy if there are too many in the space available. Your plant retailer can advise you. Some plants require many inches of water above their roots and need to be placed in the deep-water area, while others can withstand no more than a few inches above their roots during the growing season and need to be located on a shallow ledge at the edge of the pond.

The direction in which a plant grows is also important. Some plants grow vertically, up and out of the water, while others spread over or under the surface of the water. A plant's ultimate size in height or width must be taken into account to be certain that your pond will provide enough growing room.

Hardy water lilies are beautiful, spreading plants that require deep water for vigor during the summer and survival through the winter.

Water lily leaves are used as aquatic "benches" by many kinds of animals, from frogs such as this Pickerel Frog to insects such as ants and spiders.

They come in an assortment of colors that will delight your eyes and make it difficult to choose just one variety if your pond is small. Luckily, there are water lilies whose growth habit is limited, so you should be able to find one that your pond can accommodate. Water lilies send out rafts of floating leaves on which frogs, spiders, and even water striders sometimes rest, providing you with easy views of these pond visitors or inhabitants. Songbirds may even land on a water lily pad to get a drink. An important reason to buy a water lily (these plants are expensive, but they live for many years) is to provide some shade so that the water does not get too hot for the animals living in it. Locating your pond in a spot that gets mid- to late-afternoon shade is also a good way to prevent the water from overheating.

You also need to have some submergent plants that grow underneath the water's surface. They provide oxygen to many of the animals living in the pond, such as worms. Anacharis resembles seaweed and grows so well in small ponds that you usually have to remove some of it every year. You can place the excess around your garden plants as mulch or add it to the compost pile.

You should definitely grow at least one vertical plant in your pond to provide a place for dragonfly and damselfly naiads to climb up out of the water and molt into their adult forms. I have found thalias, cattails, and flags to be good plants for this purpose. Tall plants also add visual interest to a pond.

Within a few weeks of setting up your pond, you will probably begin to see signs of animal life. Insects, such as water striders that skate on the surface, will fly in from other bodies of water. Newts and frogs that discover your pond just by wandering around will float near the surface or peek up out of the depths.

Many folks worry about artificial ponds serving as breeding grounds for mosquitoes, but this is not a problem in a natural garden. An adult female mosquito looking for a place to lay her eggs finds standing water in tree holes, temporary puddles formed in animal tracks or in areas of slow-draining soil, or in still ponds. Manmade breeding grounds such as clogged gutters, flowerpot saucers, children's swimming pools, and tarps that contain standing water also contribute to the presence of mosquitoes around homes. Depending on the species, eggs might be laid singly or as a floating raft of eggs. The eggs hatch very quickly, usually within two weeks (depending on species and temperature). In these situations, mosquito eggs and larvae are subject to predation. Birds obtaining water from tree-hole puddles slurp up mosquito eggs and young. Amphibians roaming around on the ground at night find the maturing mosquitoes and eat them. Newts, dragonfly and damselfly larvae, and predacious beetles in ponds take advantage of floating mosquito meals. So as long as you have these natural mosquito controls around your pond, mosquitoes are kept in check.

Some folks put in small artificial ponds mainly to enjoy goldfish or koi—hardy nonnative (Asian) fish that can remain in the pond year-round. Inevitably, when you turn a pond into an outdoor aquarium, you are creating a "restaurant" for wildlife in the area. You cannot expect fish-eating animals such as Great Blue Herons, raccoons, and snakes to ignore the easy pickings. Some folks put fencing around their ponds to keep predators out, but this detracts from the beauty of the pond. If

If you put Goldfish into your artificial pond, you may be tempted to treat it as an outdoor aquarium. Please do not. Artificial ponds become homes to numerous species of wildlife that you will kill if you use chemicals or empty it for scrubbing.

A little Northern Water Snake lived in the author's artificial pond for two seasons. Contrary to what people expected, it did not have a serious impact upon the populations of any of the wildlife, including the Goldfish.

Tadpoles are scavengers until they grow big enough to really function as predators. They and other animals will help to keep the pond clean for you by feeding upon (and thereby recycling) dead animals like this little Snapping Turtle.

you just allow the pond to function naturally, your fish will reproduce and maintain or even increase their numbers. Indeed, if other animals do not thin their ranks by feeding on them (see chapter 6) the fish population could easily become too large. And fish that live in overcrowded conditions will ultimately succumb to disease.

When you purchase fish for your pond, you may be encouraged to buy large blackish-colored snails. These nonnative snails are sold to help clean up the pond by feeding on waste products. You can safely resist the sales pitch. Native organisms, such as worms, will move into your pond free of charge to fulfill that function. And after frogs have mated, their tadpoles will help keep the pond in tip-top shape by feeding upon animals that die in the pond. Your artificial pond will quickly become a miniature ecosystem.

Although it may be nice to use a pump to circulate pond water, whether to help aerate the water or to incorporate a stream into the pond design, a pump is not a necessary element. It is easier on your wallet and on the environment (the use of energy results in pollution) to put in a pumpless pond. However, a pond without a pump should definitely be situated where it will receive afternoon shade to reduce daytime heating.

When artificial ponds are maintained in an ecologically correct manner, they can function as ponds in the truest sense of the word. Native wildlife that moves in will create a natural ecosystem (interdependent organisms and the environment they depend upon) that is almost self-sustaining. Therefore, you should not treat your pond like an aquarium that needs a great deal of maintenance. Ignore the instructions to remove everything from the pond each fall in order to scrub down the walls and bottom surfaces of the pond. People who do this end up wondering where all the wildlife went. The sad answer is that when they cleaned their ponds, they threw out the baby (wildlife) with the bath (pond) water.

Remove as many free-floating leaves and stems as possible, but do not worry about getting every bit of plant debris out. Remember, the debris that settles to the bottom of the pond will decay into a nutrient-rich muck, providing a place for animals (where I live, Green Frogs and tadpoles) to hibernate out of sight of active year-round predators. Let the muck build up for a few years, until it has become more than a few inches deep. You should then remove some of the muck with a plastic measuring cup (glass might break). Carefully push the cup down to the bottom and gently scoop up some muck. Bring the cup back to the surface *very* slowly to avoid dispersing the muck through the water. The pond will inevitably become cloudy from the disturbance, making it difficult to see the bottom. If you need to remove more than one cup of material, you may want to wait for the water to clear up so you can see what you are doing.

Pour the muck into a plastic tub and wait a few minutes before checking it carefully for any animals. This gives the critters a chance to make themselves apparent by their movement. If you find something—even if you do not recognize it—put it back into the pond. Remember that all animals have a function. The nutrient-rich muck that remains in the tub can be placed around your plants. Fresh out of the pond, the muck is smelly, but its essence quickly dissipates.

After several years, you will probably need to remove some of the plants from your pond. Over time, plants may escape the confines of their pots and begin to take up too much room. The easiest way to deal with an overgrown plant is to pull as much of it as possible out of the water and onto the edge of the pond. Use a sharp knife to cut through the growth beyond the pot and then carefully return only the potted plant to the pond.

When spring comes, algae will start to build up in the pond, and the water may become quite green. People tend to jump to the conclusion that something is wrong, but in fact, this greening up of your pond is natural and necessary. It is needed for the influx of amphibians that will

The growth of algae in your pond in spring is normal. It is nature's way of providing food for the many young amphibians that will be born.

mate and leave their fertilized eggs, eventually hatching many hundreds of offspring that could not survive without algae to eat.

Note that overfeeding the fish in your pond will keep algae abundant throughout the warm months. To avoid this, feed fish very little or not at all. Fish should be able to survive on naturally available foods.

Keep in mind that your artificial pond should be treated like a natural pond that possesses its own system of checks and balances. Never add chemicals to this dynamic and living system.

Keeping Water from Freezing

Whether you have a birdbath or a pond, it is a good idea to heat the water during freezing weather so wildlife has access to this vital liquid year-round.

The easiest way to keep water in a birdbath unfrozen is to buy one that has a heater in the base. Submersible deicers are also available; these heating elements are placed into the birdbath. In order to use a heated birdbath or a deicing unit, your birdbath must be located near an electrical outlet where it can be plugged in. The outlet should be grounded, preferably on a ground-fault circuit interrupter for safety.

Unless you are vigilant about keeping the water from freezing, you should probably empty a concrete birdbath and store it for the winter, because concrete can crack. Make sure that it is completely dry before storing it. You can either store the birdbath indoors or leave it covered outside. If you choose to do the latter, place the dish leaning on the side of the pedestal and cover both parts with a large plastic trash bag. Weigh down the edges of the bag with bricks or rocks so that it will not blow away.

Small artificial ponds can also employ deicers. If your pond is not located near the house and an appropriate outlet, hire a licensed electrician to bring a wire from your circuit box to the vicinity of the pond where an outlet can be installed.

For preformed artificial ponds, a 250-watt or smaller heating element will do just fine. Ignore the information on the box that says that the heater is made for containers up to twenty-five gallons in size (your pond is much larger than this). The manufacturer is assuming that you want a heater capable of keeping that entire volume of water unfrozen, but your goal is different. You need to maintain only a small opening of liquid water in your pond. This opening will prevent carbon dioxide and methane (which result from metabolic processes and decomposition) from building up. Otherwise, these gases could asphyxiate wildlife living in the pond. The opening in the ice will introduce oxygen into the water, in addition to allowing land-dwelling animals to get a drink.

You should not use a large heating element that will warm the water in the entire pond. Cold water is necessary for animals (including fish) to either hibernate or enter a state of torpor (slowed metabolism). Animals that remain active would require food that is not readily available during the winter.

I place my heating element on a brick that I put on an underwater shelf at the edge of my pond. This positions the heater just a few inches under the surface of the water to keep it warmer than the freezing air above. Be sure that the deicer is thermostatically controlled (to keep the water temperature in the 35- to 45-degree range). Then you will not have to worry about removing the deicer on warm days when running it would waste energy and money.

Chapter 6

Accepting Predators

As recently as October 1989, gamekeepers on a private estate in Virginia were found to be illegally killing hawks and owls. The gamekeepers were from Europe, as was their wealthy employer, and they were following a centuries-old tradition.

Hundreds of years ago, people with lots of money kept an unnaturally high population of game, both birds and mammals, within the confines of their estates. They hired gamekeepers whose job was to manage these animals so that the owners could hunt with success whenever they felt like engaging in this "sport." Naturally, many kinds of predators were attracted to these dense concentrations of animals, because the overcrowded conditions made it easier for them to hunt successfully as well. But this posed a problem for the gamekeepers. The natural predators (such as owls, hawks, and foxes) became serious competitors.

All creatures are struggling to survive, but unfortunately, humans have an advantage over the rest of the animal kingdom. Human beings tend to use their power without comprehending its consequences. And, generally speaking, the human inclination has always been to condemn other creatures for doing what comes naturally to them.

Thus, gamekeepers labeled the predatory animals vermin. All animals that somehow harmed people and were considered difficult to control acquired this name, along with the connotation that such creatures were "bad" and should therefore be destroyed. Humankind's feeling of superiority obscured the importance of each species' contribution to the proper functioning of the environment.

Large groups of migrating Broad-winged Hawks can easily be seen in certain areas of the United States from late summer to early fall. These hawks are forced to leave northern areas when their main food sources, amphibians and reptiles, disappear by going into hibernation.

In America, this kind of thinking persists to some extent, although some animals are now protected by law. Thus, hundreds of thousands of migrating hawks are no longer slaughtered by hunters, as they were through the first decades of the twentieth century, nor are resident hawks routinely killed by farmers protecting their chickens.

In addition, most state fish and game departments have discontinued the bounty system, whereby people were rewarded with money for killing animals (such as wolves) that had been labeled "pests" by these government entities. Unfortunately, the U.S. Department of Agriculture still allows such killing when enough people complain, even when the "problem" is the result of poor management practices rather than an overpopulation of a particular species of predator. Sadder still is the labeling of an animal as pestiferous when its presence is simply misunderstood or when such labeling is employed as a means to collect money (some states reimburse farmers for animals killed by predators).

Generally, people are repelled by predation, yet their aversion is puzzlingly selective. The killing and eating of one animal by another is often viewed with distaste by people, even though, unless they are vegetarians, they do the same thing indirectly (thanks to slaughterhouses). And most folks do not feel bad for the insect or spider caught by a bird to feed to its young, yet they feel terrible if a hawk makes a meal of a bird at a feeder or a snake feeds on eggs in a nest.

Sharp-shinned Hawks feed mainly upon birds and should therefore be expected to visit bird feeders. Grow shrubbery or place brush piles nearby as an escape route for healthy birds, and the hawks will tend to catch only those birds that are less alert or sickly.

It is understandable that people feel protective of the birds they lure into their yards with food, and losing one to a hawk can be upsetting. And most people would rather not witness a snake feeding upon songbird chicks in a box put out for the purpose of helping the parents find a safe place to nest. Yet we must use our brains as well as our hearts when we alter the environment around us. Whether you put out food or nesting boxes for the entertainment of bird watching or because you want to assist wildlife, you must accept that predation is a vital part of the natural world.

For example, I enjoy the company of a pair of Carolina Wrens living around my house. They take shelter every winter in a box on my porch that I put up for that purpose, and they nest every spring and summer on shelves placed for their convenience in my carport. I adore these little birds, and I am heartbroken if any of their nesting attempts fails. Yet if all of the offspring of the Carolina Wrens survived, my yard and the surrounding area would quickly be overwhelmed. In the southeastern United States where I live, a Carolina Wren pair typically nests three times from spring through summer, averaging four eggs per nesting. Thus, one pair could produce twelve more Carolina Wrens by the end of summer. Without predation and other sources of mortality, this one pair of Carolina Wrens could be the source of *565 million* Carolina Wrens in just ten years if all of the individuals survived and reproduced year after year. Obviously, the environment could not support that many birds—and this is the result of only one pair in one yard!

Predation occurs all around us every day. If you do not pay much attention to the natural world, you will not be particularly aware of the lives and deaths of the numerous organisms around you. But the moment you start to closely observe the creatures residing in or passing through your yard, you cannot help but notice that some animals make it through the day and others do not. We cannot play the part of a prejudiced god who protects only particular types or species of wildlife. What we can and should do is to take our environmental responsibilities seriously by making our yard alterations imitative of the natural world. In this way, our enticements to wildlife will prove more beneficial than detrimental.

Protecting Feeders and Nest Boxes

The act of predation usually serves to remove sick and weak organisms from the environment to make room for healthy organisms that can reproduce. More often than not, hawks are unsuccessful when they try to attack healthy animals. Thus, healthy birds with an escape route from the feeding area that shields them from the hawk's view are apt to avoid becoming a meal. If you are witnessing hawk attacks that are frequently successful, you have not provided sufficient nearby cover. Either plant shrubs or create a brush pile at least nine feet away from the feeder. This distance will prevent squirrels from using the shrubs or brush as a jumping-off point to the feeder.

Keeping snakes and other predators, such as raccoons, from devouring eggs or young birds in nest boxes is a more difficult task. Some boxes can be placed on poles with baffles that prevent climbing animals from making their way up to the box at the top. However, for a baffle to work, the pole has to be at least five to six feet tall; otherwise, the animal might be able to jump over the baffle directly from the ground. You should *never* put grease or any other kind of sticky deterrent on poles to prevent predators from climbing them. An animal may be unable to remove the substance from its body and, in the process of trying to do so, is likely to ingest it. This could endanger the animal's life.

Placing boxes on poles works only for bird species (such as bluebirds and chickadees) that nest within about six feet off the ground. For birds that nest at greater heights, such as screech-owls and Great Crested Fly-catchers, boxes have to be placed directly on large trees. In this case, there is no way to place a protective baffle without harming the tree.

If your yard and the local environment are in a fairly natural state, so that predators have an abundance of food choices, your boxes should fledge young birds more often than not. There is no reason to expect an artificial nesting cavity to be more attractive to predators than natural openings in trees. If, however, the birds using your nest box seem to experience excessive mortality, take down the box and place it somewhere else. If you think you know what made the box vulnerable, try to correct the situation. Perhaps it was too close to the ground or too near another plant or object that a predator could use to easily reach the box.

Another possibility is that your neighborhood is simply too "clean." If there are no dead trees for cavity-nesting animals to use and no one else in the neighborhood has bird boxes, a lone nesting box in your yard could be an obvious invitation to predators. You could try to get your neighbors interested in putting up boxes. Most people enjoy seeing birds, and some might really get into this activity, although you should discuss predation with them and remind them that the boxes need to be cleaned out at least once a year to prevent parasite infestations.

If you cannot get the neighbors interested in accommodating wildlife or find a safe site in your yard, you may have to forgo putting out nesting boxes until the local environment improves. Although we need to accept predation as a necessary element of life, we do not need to create situations that make animals vulnerable.

Controlling Domestic Predators

Many people think that there is nothing wrong with dogs and cats catching wildlife; they feel it is their nature to hunt and that these pets are no different from native predators. But pets—as well as feral cats and dogs—are very different. First, there are not enough prey species to support both the huge number of pets in this country and the number of native predators that are totally dependent upon their prey for survival. Pets have not been taken into account in the natural scheme of things. Thus, predation by pets results in added pressure on both prey and predator species, which could doom some of them to extinction.

Second, pets that are well cared for are not killing to survive. Native predators, in contrast, are in a life-or-death struggle every day to get enough food. Every animal that a pet kills is one that cannot be caught and eaten by a wild creature whose very existence depends upon it.

Cats and dogs should never be employed to control wildlife around homes, farms, or businesses. Because these animals are not selective, they will kill many other kinds of animals besides the ones you want limited.

Nonselective killing should always be avoided because the cost to the environment (and ultimately to us as well as other species) is too high.

In addition, a roaming dog or cat may inadvertently cause the deaths of numerous young animals if it keeps a mother off her nest. Young animals need to be fed regularly and kept warm if the weather is cool.

Thus, the best thing you can do for your wildlife is to keep your pets indoors and to supervise them when they are outdoors. You should call animal control to pick up any strays.

Chapter 7

Observing Wildlife

Once you have recognized the value—and ease—of living in agreement with nature, you will be able to enjoy the natural world because you realize that it is not the enemy. To get the most out of your wildlife preserve, you will have to be observant. By carefully checking out your surroundings, you will learn to recognize the many kinds of wildlife that have taken advantage of your efforts.

Bird Watching

Some kinds of animals are easier to see than others because they can be directed to a particular spot in the yard where it is convenient to observe them. For example, if you place bird feeders in a location near a window, you will be able to look out at them every time you walk by or take a seat near the window. Your window will become an entertainment center of sorts as you watch the various seed-eating birds that have been attracted to your offerings.

Many people enjoy watching birds because they tend to be colorful, many of them sing lovely songs, and they are probably the easiest kinds of wildlife to observe anywhere in the world. You will enjoy this pastime more if you purchase a regional field guide to help you identify the birds you see at your feeders and around your yard. Once you make an identification, you can increase your knowledge by doing some research in other books or online. There are numerous field guides available, and my philosophy is that you can never have too many field guides. For example, sometimes the picture of a particular species is better in one book than in another, and that can make the difference between successfully identifying a bird and being left confused about what you saw. Some books point out the features (such as wing bars or breast spotting) that, if present, can clinch an identification. This system is extremely useful, even for more experienced birders.

Some kinds of birds do not eat at seed feeders, so you will have to do other things to entice them to visit. You will also have to look more carefully for them. To bring fruit-eating birds to your property, plant fruit-bearing shrubs and trees. After the fruits have formed, keep an eye on the ripening process. Check the plants as often as you can each day once the fruits are nearly ripe. This maximizes the possibility that you will look out at just the right moment to see one or more birds fly in to feast on the fruits that you grew especially for them.

If you can view the plants from inside the house, approach the window slowly so that you do not startle any birds that might be feeding. Any sudden movement will probably frighten them away. If you must go outside to check the plants, walk slowly until you are just close enough for a view. Birds will get nervous and fly away if they are aware of your presence. Of course, many mammals eat fruit too, and as a bonus, you may get to see them as well.

Pond Watching

If you have an artificial pond, birds and mammals will come to it for a drink of water or perhaps to feed upon the pond's inhabitants (see chapter 6 for a discussion of the importance of predation). You will also entice many reptiles and amphibians to visit or inhabit your watery oasis.

To really get to know the life within a pond, you need to actually visit the pond instead of just looking at it from inside the house, even if it is near a window. You may be amazed to find some animals swimming underwater even on the coldest days of winter. And if you go outside at night with a flashlight to take a quick peek (sustained light is disturbing to the animals) into the water, you might be surprised by what you see.

I discovered this by accident one evening because I wanted to show my husband the new Wood Frog eggs in our pond. He got home after sundown, so I went outside with a flashlight to illuminate the egg mass for him. To my surprise, several predaceous diving beetles—animals I had seldom spotted in my ponds during the daylight hours—were actively swimming around the Wood Frog egg mass. Not only were there more of these insects than I had ever realized were in the pond, but

I also discovered that they fed upon the jellylike substance that envelops the Wood Frog eggs!

During the warm months of the year, it is best to sneak up on a pond. Frogs, snakes, or salamanders that may be resting along the edges will usually dive into the water as soon as they sense a person nearby, but sometimes you get lucky, and an animal is brave enough to stay put.

A pond can teach you to be a keen observer, because sometimes you will not know that an animal is present until it splashes into the water. Then you realize that you should have looked harder at the surroundings as you approached, and you vow to do better next time. It is also a good idea to bring binoculars along so that you can see the pond area from a distance.

Green Frogs are common in Virginia and seem to eventually recognize people that spend time at their pond. Once that happens, they will stay put as you approach instead of jumping into the water.

Yard Watching

When walking around your yard, always keep your eyes open. A Box Turtle may be plodding along, or a little Red Eft (the immature terrestrial form of the Eastern Newt) may be boldly searching for insects to eat. You would not want to step on these animals and hurt them because you weren't paying attention.

This strategy will help you avoid stepping on a snake, too. Although many snakes are active mostly at

A Red Eft is more likely to be seen wandering around following a rain storm.

night, they may be out and about during daylight hours. They will usually try to stay out of sight, because they are as afraid of humans as we tend to be of them. However, one may cross your path, so it is a good idea to keep your eyes open.

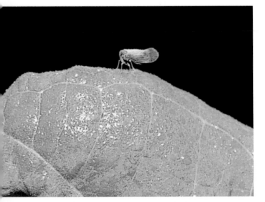

This plant hopper, small but sporting a lovely blue color, could be easily overlooked by the wildlife watcher who is not alert to the tiniest wildlife around him.

People rarely think of insect, spider, and other invertebrate life-forms as wildlife, but these little creatures can be fascinating. Many invertebrates are easily found, while others may require careful searching. A close look at your plants may reveal diminutive critters that are strangers to you. There are books to help you identify them and find out about their lives.

Wherever you observe wildlife, please keep in mind that you should not harass it. Look only briefly; even insects and spiders perceive possible threats.

Chance Encounters

Look out your windows as often as you can, because you never know what might be out there. A benefit of watching wildlife from inside is that you can often observe an animal for a longer time. As long as the animal does not notice you, it will not be frightened away. Therefore, you may get to see how an animal hunts or what it eats.

One afternoon, a Gray Fox came to my yard while Gray Squirrels were eating sunflower seeds beneath a bird feeder. I watched the fox crouch low and then stealthily approach the feeding area. But alas for the

The Gray Fox, an animal that normally starts hunting at dusk, may hunt during the daytime if it feels safe. Nocturnal animals found hunting during the day are probably not rabid unless they are acting ill and do not look well.

fox, the squirrels somehow got wind of it and scurried up some nearby trees, where they barked and whined about the intruder.

Sometimes an animal may be just inches away from your window, and if you keep the glass clean, inside and out, you can actually take photographs through the window for documentation and identification. One afternoon, a Gray Treefrog was grasping the trunk of the privet that grows in front of my kitchen window, and I got its picture. On another occasion, I noticed one of these amphibians right outside my living room window, just taking it easy, lying in the sunshine on the nearby porch railing.

The Gray Treefrog is normally found on trees and shrubs, but you may also discover one resting on your porch railing.

One morning as my husband and I were eating breakfast, I happened to look through my office window that faces the front yard. At my request, my husband had recently "planted" a snag there, which I had drilled holes into and filled with peanut butter for the birds to eat. To my surprise, a big American Black Bear was ambling down the driveway

The American Black Bear is becoming more common in certain areas. If you live in bear country, help these large animals to be better-behaved neighbors by preventing them from associating food with humans.

toward the snag. I immediately yelled "A bear!" and ran for my camera and tripod. I normally do not enjoy having my breakfast interrupted, but it is always exciting to see one of these big mammals.

You should also check your yard at dusk. Many animals become active at this time of day, so you may spot something unusual. Just as it was getting dark one evening, I looked through the big window into my front yard before I put the light on. To my surprise, a Gray Fox was eating sunflower chips that had fallen onto the ground under a bird feeder.

Wildlife sightings are made by those who consciously try to be observant. This normally nocturnal Southern Flying Squirrel was peeking out of one of the author's wildlife boxes during the daytime.

Another day around dusk, I was in my kitchen looking through the sliding glass doors, watching as the bats started to fly around catching insects. As I looked toward the west side of my yard, where a bird box was situated high on a tree, I noticed that the entrance hole of the bird box had "disappeared." I grabbed my binoculars for a better look and discovered a Southern Flying Squirrel—a nocturnal animal—in the hole, ready to exit the box. I watched nearly every evening for the rest of the summer to see the squirrel leaving the box.

So do not let your windows go to waste. They are there to let the light in and to give you a view of the outside world. If you do not look out every chance you get, you may be missing a wonderful wildlife pageant.

Finally, pay attention to sounds, and whenever you hear an unfamiliar one, check it out. Early one evening, just after dark, I heard a thump on my deck. I quickly shut off the inside light, put on the deck light, and peered out. I was absolutely delighted to spot a little red Eastern Screech-Owl (some Eastern Screech-Owls are grayish brown) on the deck railing. Although it wasn't entirely clear what it had done to make the sound I had heard, I am certain that the little owl was hunting out there. It may have been after a mouse feeding on birdseed spilled from my deck feeders. Or the owl may have been after one of the birds that often roost in the large bushes that line my deck. Whatever the little owl was after, it gave me the extraordinary opportunity to see it out in the open, where its small size (about eight and a half inches tall) was very apparent.

Missed opportunities can also be instructive. One day, as I was writing my newspaper column, I heard the local Tufted Titmouse family making a subdued racket, indicating that a predator was in the yard, but nothing that presented a serious and imminent danger to the birds, such as a fox. (After you have listened to birds long enough, you can actually tell what kind of predator is around by how upset they sound.) I was feeling pressed for time, but I did get up and take a quick look outside. Nothing was visible, so I returned to my writing and forgot about the titmice. When my husband got home from work, he asked if I had seen the big snakeskin at the edge of the carport. I could have kicked myself. I realized that I had missed an opportunity to watch a Black Rat Snake shed its skin! Now, no matter how busy I am, if the birds make a ruckus, I very carefully check it out.

So do pay attention by keeping your eyes and ears open. You just never know what might be awaiting you in your yard.

Selecting Binoculars

The beauty of wildlife watching is that it is an inexpensive hobby. However, there is one tool that you must own in order to get the most out of this pastime: a decent pair of binoculars. If you can afford to buy a moderate- to high-priced pair, you will obtain better (and thus more entertaining) views of wildlife. Here are some guidelines for choosing binoculars. First, consider how you plan to use the binoculars most of the time in order to determine the minimum focusing distance that you require. For example, if you want to obtain a good look at butterflies alighting on nearby plants or birds coming to feeders, you may want binoculars that can be focused on objects that are fairly close to you. This is not possible with all binoculars.

Second, consider the time of day you will usually be using the binoculars to determine the proper size objective lenses. The objective lenses are the ones opposite the eyepieces you look through. The light-gathering power of binoculars is directly proportional to the size of the objective lenses. The larger the lenses, the more light-gathering power the binoculars possess. If you plan to spend a lot of time looking for animals

Butterflies like this Spicebush Swallowtail will land much closer to human watchers than birds usually will. If your main hobby is butterfly watching, you may want to buy binoculars that focus as close to you as possible.

in dim light (such as owls or foxes that become active at dusk), you will want larger objective lenses than if you are interested in nature watching on bright, sunny days. If you want to engage in both (as I do), you might compromise by buying binoculars with objective lenses sized toward the middle range of diameters available. You should not purchase binoculars with bigger lenses than you truly need. Bigger lenses increase the size and weight of binoculars, which may make them more difficult to use.

Third, do not be swayed by the common misconception that a higher power of magnification is always better. Seven-, eight-, or nine-power binoculars make your subject appear to be that many times closer to you. Any one of these magnifications is usually sufficient for identification purposes. Keep in mind the following points when considering how high a magnification you want: The higher the magnification of the binoculars, the smaller the field of view. The field of view is measured in degrees, and it tells you how much of the area around your subject will be visible when you look through the eyepieces. The higher the number, the larger the area you can see. A smaller field of view makes it more difficult to find your object of interest, because you have to pinpoint its location more accurately when you raise the binoculars to your eyes. For example, if you cannot immediately locate an animal high in a fully leafed tree, a smaller field of view necessitates more searching around to cover the animal's possible location, whereas a larger field of view would allow you to view a greater area all at once. Also, you will have more difficulty trying to get a look at an animal that is on the move if your binoculars have a small field of view. Again, your "aim" will have to be more accurate as you try to get the animal in your sights.

Ten-power binoculars are quite popular with serious bird-watchers. However, with this power of magnification, unless you can hold your binoculars very steady, the image will jiggle and you will not have a decent view, regardless of the magnification.

Fourth, do some research by reading magazine articles that evaluate binoculars. Ask your friends what they like and dislike about the binoculars they own. Then try out as many models as possible by reputable manufacturers. Read the accompanying literature, which should include the minimum focusing distance (usually nine to fifteen feet, but some may focus down to three to six feet), the weight of the model, and the size of the field of view. Check the various combinations of magnification and objective lens size (given as two numbers, such as 9x30). Hold the binoculars to see how they feel in your hands. Some binoculars may be too big for small hands, or they may be too heavy for you. If you wear eyeglasses, make sure that the binoculars are comfortable. Also check the focusing mechanism to see how quickly you can set the focus. Birds and other wildlife usually do not linger for long.

You may have to make some compromises, because no one pair of binoculars will do everything you want it to. Or you might consider buying more than one pair (for example, two moderately priced binoculars instead of one expensive pair) if you are serious about activities that require different specifications. If you want to identify both butterflies and birds, you could buy one pair of binoculars that focuses down to six feet or less for butterfly watching (butterflies usually land much closer to people than birds do) and another that focuses down to nine feet or more for bird watching.

Another benefit of owning more than one pair of binoculars is that you will be able to keep a pair near every window you tend to look out of a lot. Having binoculars handy when you spot an animal can make the difference between getting a good look and making an identification and not knowing for sure what it was you glimpsed.

If you purchase binoculars from a well-known maker of quality optical equipment, you can hardly go wrong. Binoculars are precision instruments, so you probably should spend a minimum of $200. If this seems like a lot of money, remember that with good care, your binoculars should last a lifetime—and more. I still have my father's binoculars that were given to me many decades ago. They still function, and they bring back many fond memories.

Chapter 8

Recording Your Observations

Many bird-watchers keep lists of the birds they see, and serious gardeners usually keep track of their successes and failures with plants. However, few people take notes about the other kinds of natural events that occur in their yards or elsewhere, but everyone could learn a great deal by getting into the habit of doing so.

Making notes comes easily to me, because I was born with a scientific mind; I have always wanted to learn as much as possible about nature. The habit of taking notes transformed me from a person with just an interest in the natural world to a person with enough knowledge to begin writing about it—and to become a "voice" for wildlife.

For example, after my first little pond was installed, I immediately started to keep track of the various animals I saw in and around it, along with dates, times of day, weather conditions, and detailed accounts of their activities. A few years later, I read an article published in a university gardening newsletter that advised people to completely clean out their artificial ponds every fall—remove all the water, scrub down the interior surfaces, refill the pond with fresh water, and put back the plants and fish. The article did not take into consideration the wildlife that might have moved into such ponds.

I immediately wrote an article about the deleterious effects on wildlife that such a thorough pond cleaning would have, such as the killing of dragonfly and damselfly naiads as a result of removing pond water. I explained how getting rid of the muck at the bottom of the pond would make it impossible for frogs to hibernate. I made it clear why it was important *not* to clean a pond in such a manner and why it was actually unnecessary to perform this task. My article was published, undoubtedly after the horticulturist-editor made sure that I had my facts straight.

When an acquaintance of mine (who had owned a pond for many more years than I had) heard about my article, he asked what made me "such an expert" after having a pond for only a few years. How could I know so much more than he knew? The answer was that I had paid closer attention to my pond and I had given much more thought to my pond observations. I had made notes and learned from them.

Identification and Research

You can begin to learn about wildlife by first accurately identifying the organisms you observe in your yard. To identify wildlife, you will need guidebooks. Birds, insects, and spiders are found almost everywhere, so you should own at least one book about each of these groups. If you expect to find other kinds of wildlife in your yard, such as amphibians, reptiles, and mammals, you should also have books about them.

The little Golden Guides that I grew up using are wonderful for making wildlife identifications. If you buy all of the Golden Guide books devoted to animals, you will be off to a good start. However, you will likely need more than just one guidebook for making insect and spider identifications. There are so many species that no one book can illustrate all of them.

After I identify an organism, I read about it in more detail. I then compare what I read to what I recorded in my notes. I have discovered that my observations do not always jibe with what is written in other sources. These discrepancies have made me aware that sometimes bad information gets published. That information is repeated by subsequent authors who are consulting other sources instead of relying on their own observations. Constantly repeated erroneous information eventually becomes accepted as "fact."

An example of such misinformation is that sunflower seed shells left on the ground by birds at feeders are allelopathic, meaning that they release a substance that inhibits the germination or growth of other plants. My observations suggest that there is no harmful substance exuded from sunflower seed shells; rather, the quantity of shells may present a physical barrier (like a thick layer of mulch) to plants trying to grow up through it. I have seen many kinds of flowering plants that managed to grow through a thick covering of sunflower seed shells, making a strong case against sunflower seed shells being allelopathic. The origin of the myth is likely the fact that lawn grass invariably suffers when too many sunflower seed shells accumulate on it. But the grass would be smothered by any kind of thick mulch placed over it. Grass blades are just not strong enough to push mulch aside. The blades begin to die and rot underneath sunflower shells, just as they would underneath any kind of mulch that prevented sunlight from reaching them.

When you make your own detailed observations of the natural world, you will have a better idea of which information you can trust as being accurate. We are living in an age when information can be obtained almost effortlessly, but unfortunately, not all information is good information. If you follow poor advice, you may harm not only wildlife but also the natural workings of your garden.

Observation Versus Interpretation

The most important aspect of taking notes is to accurately record exactly what you see, without any interpretations or inferences—unless you clearly distinguish between observations and interpretations.

For example, in my younger years, I once observed a Peregrine Falcon standing outside my window. It held an adult male Purple Finch pinned against the ground under its talons. The falcon kept raising and lowering one foot and then the other as it looked around. I assumed that this repeated foot-raising was a sign that the finch was still alive and perhaps struggling under the bird's talons. I later shared my observation with a knowledgeable bird-watcher, stating that the finch *was* alive rather than that I had *wondered* whether the finch were alive because of the falcon's foot movements. Her response—that the finch had almost certainly been dead—made me realize that I had related my assumption as if it were fact. But I had never seen the finch move.

Ever since that day, I have been extremely careful not to turn my assumptions into "facts," whether jotting down notes or relaying my experiences in writing or face-to-face. You must beware of falling into this trap, but remember, everyone makes mistakes. If you do goof, just fess up and set the record straight. Feigning knowledge that you do not have, or inadvertently misleading someone and then failing to correct the error, is far worse than admitting that you slipped up.

For example, I once read a newspaper column that encouraged folks to make bat houses out of treated wood. I knew that the chemicals in the wood could harm the young animals and perhaps the adults if it leached out of the wood, and I asked the columnist to retract his suggestion, but it was rather difficult to get him to do so. There should be no shame in making a correction, but one should be ashamed for deliberately failing to do so. Providing such misinformation can have serious consequences for our natural world.

Using Observations to Plan for the Future

It is important to date your observations and note weather conditions, because you never know when they might be relevant. For example, I discovered that Gray Treefrogs often call during the summer just before a thunderstorm. And Spring Peepers (another kind of treefrog) might call at any time of the year when the temperatures are somewhat cool and the air is a bit damp—just as it is in spring, when these tiny frogs mate.

By paying attention to the calls of the treefrogs, I can figure out when there is a good possibility of rain. This allows me to time the application of fertilizer or lime. Because these substances need to be "rained in," it is less work for me and less of a demand upon water resources if I can spread them just before a rain shower. Fertilizer and lime should not be allowed to remain on the soil surface for long. Unwatered fertilizer loses its nitrogen to the atmosphere, and birds might ingest fertilizer granules, mistaking them for seeds.

Sometimes it is helpful to know the time of day that wildlife events occur so that you can prepare for them. For instance, over the course of many years, I have noted which species of birds are the first ones up in the morning. Therefore, I know when I need to have their food in place so that they can eat right away. And by paying attention to the kinds of foods particular bird species prefer, I know what to serve them.

In winter, Mourning Doves, White-throated Sparrows, Dark-eyed Juncos, and Northern Cardinals are poking around on the ground when it is barely light enough to see. In summer, Eastern Towhees replace the sparrows and juncos that have gone north, joining the doves and cardinals. All of these birds eat white millet and cracked corn, which I make sure are well stocked in my feeder trays the evening before.

In contrast, my resident male Carolina Wren is something of a late riser. I know when he starts the day because he sings a "good morning" song shortly after emerging from his sleeping spot (usually a shelf in my carport or a shelter box on my porch). His mate twitters in response, and the two of them usually get up together. The wrens enjoy eating peanut butter, so it is important that this nourishing food be available in the morning, especially in winter, which is hard on Carolina Wrens. But because they do not get up quite as early as some of the other birds, I can sleep in a bit longer.

It is interesting to note that the first birds to get up in the morning may be the last ones to disappear at night. Just as a cardinal is usually the first avian creature I hear in the early morning, before it is very light out, a cardinal is usually the last bird chirping as darkness falls.

Although the wren pair gets up later in the morning, they retire by late afternoon, especially in the winter. They are rarely out and about after the sun has started to get low in the western sky. Perhaps these active little birds require more sleep than other species to recoup their energy. Or it may be that Carolina Wrens do not see well in dim light.

Paying attention to wildlife can also help you plan when to plant your vegetables. I know that I can start a spring garden about six weeks after I hear or perhaps see the first Canada Geese migrating north. Commonly traveling in large V-shaped flocks from early evening through the night and into the early morning, they start flying over my house sometime in February. I get goose bumps (no pun intended) when I hear their honking as they approach. It thrills me to think that spring is just around the corner when these big birds start leaving southern climes. For me, a large V of migrating Canada Geese—flying high above the ground, rushing to their destination so many miles away—epitomizes the meaning of the word *awesome*.

Migrating Canada Geese fly very high above the ground, often honking as they head due north.

A male cowbird bathes in the author's front yard, announcing—much as the appearance of a robin does—that spring has arrived.

Although many people equate spring with the American Robin, the Brown-headed Cowbird tells me when that season has arrived. Although cowbirds are supposedly in my area all year, I see them only from around March 20 (the spring equinox) through the first half of July. I enjoy spotting the first male cowbird, with his beautiful shiny black plumage and chocolate-brown head. But many people despise the Brown-headed Cowbird because of its breeding behavior. The female does not build a nest. Instead, she lays her eggs, usually one per site, in the nests of other bird species. Because the cowbird nestling is usually larger than the young of the host species, the cowbird chick gets most of the food brought to the nest, and the host nestlings starve. Therefore, many people blame cowbirds for the declining populations of numerous bird species in the East.

However, the true fault lies with humans, whose clearing of the virgin forests allowed these birds to move east in the first place. In the West, where the insect-eating Brown-headed Cowbird originally lived, the birds followed the American Bison from grassland to grassland eating the insects stirred up by the huge bovids. Because the cowbirds could not stay put long enough to raise their own young, they needed surrogate parents to take care of their chicks. In the West, Red-winged Blackbirds fulfilled that role without detriment to their own population. Although cowbirds do create an additional burden for endangered and threatened bird species in the East, the depletion of natural habitats due to development is a much greater cause for concern.

The Louisiana Waterthrush starts singing as March comes to a close. When I hear it, I know that migrant songbirds are on their way back and in six weeks or less, the ground should be warm enough to plant my summer crops (tomatoes, green peppers, and the like). The Great Crested Flycatcher arrives at the end of April, telling me that the danger of frost is past. And by the time Snowy Tree Crickets are singing in late August, I know that my crops will soon be petering out and that cooler weather is on the way.

Conversely, sometimes plants let me know about wildlife. When I spy tiny Small-flowered Bittercress and Persian Speedwell blooms, which require a magnifying glass to appreciate their beauty, I know that I will soon see carpenter bees, bumblebees, and bee flies on the wing. When the Pawpaw flower buds start to open in early April, looking like little maroon-and-green hearts, I know that the Whip-poor-wills will be back any day from Central America, and I should start listening for their calls as dusk falls and shortly before sunrise. And as soon as azalea blossoms start to appear in about

When Pawpaw buds are just beginning to open, they resemble little hearts that tell the author that it is time to listen for Whip-poor-wills.

mid-April, I know that I had better get my hummingbird feeders up—if I have not done so already—because most of these tiny nectar-seekers follow the azalea blooms northward. (Note that hummingbirds prefer feeders on which they can land, which allows them to conserve energy.)

When you keep accurate notes about the various wildlife events around you, day after day and year after year, you will recognize how reliable the behavior of wildlife is and how wildlife behavior relates to weather and seasonal changes. In order to survive, wild creatures need to be closely attuned to the physical world around them. They must be able to recognize when it is time to head north to mate or go south to escape harsh weather and scarce food supplies. Their arrival and departure dates may vary somewhat, but they are usually fairly consistent. If you pay attention to these comings and goings (with the help of your notes), you can predict and plan for the future.

Do Not Disturb

I am strict about not harassing wildlife, especially when young animals are involved. All wildlife should be watched (and photographed) with minimal intrusiveness to avoid disturbing it. Be alert for any behavior that indicates that you are interfering, and leave promptly.

On one occasion, a neighbor boy alerted me to a Pileated Woodpecker nest in a large, dead tree along a nearby river. He quietly and unobtrusively led me to a spot across the river from the rotting tree, where I settled in to watch and take notes. But even though I was all the way across the river and partially hidden by some shrubs, the Pileated Woodpecker parents knew that I was there. They called with alarm to their young, warning them not to peek out of the nest hole to beg for food (I had seen the chicks looking out when I first arrived). The parents stayed away from the tree, flying around in an agitated manner at some distance and calling in distress.

As soon as I witnessed this behavior, I gave up and left. If I had stayed, I would have kept the young from being fed and caused the adults unnecessary stress. Yet I still gained knowledge from my brief and distant encounter. I learned how incredibly observant these parent birds are and how well they can communicate with their young about danger. As disappointed as I was about having to leave, I still appreciated the chance to learn something about these magnificent woodpeckers. A few years later, a pair of Pileated Woodpeckers nested right on my own property. I had noticed them constantly flying back and forth over my yard and "talking" in loud voices. I knew they had to be making a nest nearby. One day as I was visiting one of my ponds, I heard the young Pileateds begging for food. The sounds led me to the nest tree, uphill from my pond. Afterward, I was able to watch from a distance as the parents took care of their family. In this case, the parents were used to seeing me in the area and did not feel that I presented a danger.

If you really want to learn about wild animals, you need to observe them without interfering with their lives. When an animal is aware of your presence, you change its behavior. To get a fascinating glimpse into the wondrous world of wildlife, always be a discreet wildlife watcher.

Chapter 9

Coexisting with Wildlife

If you want natural processes to keep your yard functioning properly, you require many species of wildlife around your home. However, sometimes wildlife can get into trouble—just as children can. Parents of young children know that they need to child-proof their homes (they would never dream of getting rid of their children). Gardeners, likewise, need to wildlife-proof their gardens, rather than trying to eliminate particular wildlife species from their environment.

The secret to helping wildlife to stay out of trouble is to acquire knowledge about the animal that is creating difficulties. Read a book and learn about the animal's habits. With such knowledge, you should be able to come up with a way to solve the problem.

White-tailed Deer

White-tailed Deer may be the most difficult creatures to deal with in the urban and suburban environment. They are found across most of the United States, but they are particularly troublesome in the East, where human beings wiped out their natural predators—the Gray Wolf and the Eastern Cougar—years ago. With these natural controls gone, White-tailed Deer have increased at the expense of other animals. They are so plentiful that trees and shrubs needed by songbirds for nest sites are being overbrowsed, impacting the birds' ability to sustain their own numbers.

It is very difficult to limit deer populations through hunting. It can be dangerous in human-congested areas, and people who are opposed to hunting often create legal roadblocks. Thus, if you live in an area where deer are competing for your food plants, you have no choice but to deal with them.

If your garden is small, your best defense may be to put up a fence. Whitetails can jump as high as eight feet, so you will need a fence taller than that. However, such a fence may create a "prison enclosure" type of atmosphere that you may not find particularly appealing.

If your garden is behind a town house or the like, you might want to build a six-foot-tall opaque wall made of wood or masonry. Deer will not jump where they cannot see. Double fencing (one three- to four-foot fence encircling a six-foot fence separated by a four-foot space hung with netting between them) also works because deer do not like to jump across large spaces, especially if there seems to be an obstacle (such as netting). The inner fence can be constructed of tall metal posts with barbed wire strung between them at the top so the netting can be draped over it.

Another less desirable option is to surround the garden with an electric fence that delivers a shock to intruding deer. This type of fencing can be very successful, but it is expensive and difficult to maintain and causes discomfort to the animal.

All of these options are costly, as well as a lot of work to install and care for. If you can withstand a bit of deer browsing, you might want to try the method I describe on page 102, which is meant only to deter smaller mammals that dig or climb.

Because fencing fruit and vegetable gardens has long been a common practice, it is a sight that people expect to see, and they do not usually consider it to be an eyesore. However, preventing deer damage to your *landscape* plants by placing fencing around them can clash with your beautification efforts. I suggest that you be realistic about your situation. Unless you want to be in a state of constant despair over your yard, give up on the plants that are deer "candy." Just as you have to accept that you cannot grow tropical plants in a temperate region, you should accept that there are certain plants that you simply cannot grow in the midst of an ever-expanding deer population.

Instead, landscape your yard with plants that are not usually eaten by deer. Determining which plants these are requires some experimentation. For example, I planted six elderberry shrubs that became absolute deer delicacies. As they grew and regrew, the deer kept devouring them. Elderberry shrubs simply did not stand a chance in my yard.

Other people will discover different deer preferences, depending on their location. Also, deer tastes may change over time. For many years, I grew quite a few varieties of daylilies in my backyard, in spite of having deer visitors. Yet some of my friends found it impossible to grow these plants. Indeed, after several years, the deer in my area started to feed voraciously upon the previously untouched daylily plants—so much so that I have rarely seen a flower in the past six years. However, the daylily plants in my front garden still bloom quite successfully, although they do receive a bit of deer browsing.

The reason that deer eat different plants in different locations, and the reason that their preferences change over time in one location, may be due to the shift in the kinds of plants available to them. A preferred plant (such as my elderberries) may eventually die out, forcing the animals to start eating something else. Therefore, you have to experiment with the expectation that, over time, your results will vary. But change is what life is all about. If you begin to lose plants to deer, consider it a golden opportunity to try something new.

However, if you prefer to have more successes than failures in the beginning, be observant. Note which kinds of plants your immediate neighbors seem to be able to grow, and buy the same kinds of plants, perhaps in different varieties or colors. Or grow the native plants that seem to do well unattended near your home.

At my home in central Virginia, abelias, azaleas, weigelas, viburnums, Mountain Laurel, Shrub Althea, Winged Euonymus, and Meideland roses are shrubs that are ignored by deer. Japanese Maple, Virginia

Because deer have no natural predators in the East, their numbers are high and gardeners do not have much choice other than to figure out how to live with them.

Fringe Tree, Flowering Dogwood, and Sourwood are smallish trees that are useful to wildlife other than deer and provide beauty in the landscape. Some flowers that deer do not seem interested in are Bee Balm or Oswego Tea, Wild Bergamot, Black-eyed Susan, Shasta Daisy, and Yarrow.

I have discovered one trick that sometimes works if you really must grow plants that deer enjoy: hide them. Summer-blooming Asiatic and Oriental lilies are deer favorites that I have grown to flowering by placing them among plants that are not touched by deer. Of course, the surrounding plants must grow at least as tall as the plant you are attempting to hide.

Another tactic when dealing with deer is simply to grow as many plants of as many kinds as possible around your house. As the deer move from area to area, they may eat less per plant, making the effects of their browsing less obvious. Keep in mind that woody plants can withstand some pruning, even pruning performed by deer.

Groundhogs, Rabbits, Raccoons, and Opossums

Small animals that are prone to digging or climbing are fairly easy to keep out of your food garden with a fence constructed from woven or metal wire (available in four- and five-foot heights) and metal fence posts. The top foot or so of fencing should not be attached to the fence posts and should be bent away from the garden at an angle of at least forty-five degrees. This loose fencing will not support the weight of animals trying to climb over it. Instead, they will fall back onto the ground.

You should also attach a two-foot-wide piece of fencing (preferably vinyl-coated) to the outside bottom of the vertical fence, lying away from the garden at a ninety-degree angle, so that it lies flat just below ground level. Cover this "apron" with a few inches of soil. Another option is to bury the bottom eighteen inches of a five-foot-tall fence. Either of these methods will deter critters from digging underneath the fencing to get to your food crops.

Of course, Groundhogs (also called Woodchucks) and the different species of rabbits are herbivorous, so if they cannot get to your food plants, they may help themselves to your flowers. If these animals live in your area, it is a good idea to grow an abundance of plants to give them something to eat. If you have numerous plants, the ones eaten by the Groundhogs and rabbits will be less noticeable.

Because I live in an area that has lots of mature hardwood forest (which is not preferred Groundhog habitat), I normally do not have Groundhogs to contend with. However, one summer, a small Groundhog (a young one, I presume) showed up and made a burrow under my porch. I watched as it chewed on my plants along the sidewalk and around the yard. I never found a plant completely eaten—or even close to it—perhaps because Groundhogs prefer grasses, clovers, and plantains. If I felt the need, I would trim up some of the dangling branches with clippers. But whether I did anything or not, all of the plants sent out new growth that made them bushier and more floriferous.

The Groundhog's burrow under my porch later sheltered a Gray Fox that had perhaps eaten the little critter. In fact, Groundhog burrows are extremely useful to many other mammals, such as rabbits, raccoons, opossums, and skunks. And some species of frogs use abandoned Groundhog burrows in which to hibernate.

Many people think of Groundhogs as nuisance animals, but these chunky little creatures perform quite a few helpful services for the environment. Their digging aerates the soil, creating pockets that give plant roots access to air and water. This digging also breaks up subsurface soil that can be transformed into topsoil when it is mixed with organic matter. Groundhog wastes are deposited in underground burrows, automatically becoming fertilizer. Groundhogs and Eastern Cottontail Rabbits also serve as food for many larger carnivorous mammals and birds. Therefore, each of these herbivorous animals is important to the survival of other species.

Sadly, the cute little bunnies loved by children somehow morph into the enemies of grown-up gardeners. This does not have to be the case. I grow hundreds of flowering plants in unfenced gardens around my

If you allow broad-leaved plants to grow in your lawn, Eastern Cottontail Rabbits might leave your expensive flowers alone, even if they are not fenced for protection.

home, and "my" cottontails do not touch them. The rabbits' lack of interest can be explained by the abundance of preferred food plants such as Common Dandelion and Common Plantain, which are available throughout my yard. Whereas most folks are trying hard to grow a green carpet of lawn that has only grass blades, my lawn, though consisting mostly of grass, also provides broadleaf plants for rabbits. The rabbits keep these plants limited in number, ensuring that my lawn is never taken over by them. And as a wonderful free bonus, I am afforded the same entertainment I so enjoyed as a child.

In addition to the leaves of dandelions and plantains, rabbits may feed on the bark of small orchard trees, especially during winter, when snow cover makes it possible for them to tunnel through the snow to the tree without being seen. The easiest way to prevent this is to shovel snow away from tree trunks after a storm. You could also place tightly woven wire fencing beyond the drip line (the imaginary line underneath the outermost tips of those tree branches from which rainwater drips) of young trunks to prevent access. Bury the bottom at least six inches below ground level, and have the top of the fence about two feet above the average snow level. Otherwise, rabbits will be able to reach the lowest limbs by hopping on the snow's surface after it hardens into a crust.

The Common Raccoon can get into more than enough trouble to make up for the lack of trouble caused by rabbits and Groundhogs. Raccoons are practically omnivorous and will consume dead or living animals as well as seeds and fruits, which is why they raid garbage cans, bird feeders, and bird nests.

Although raccoons are active mostly at night, they will sometimes venture out for a daytime snack.

An occasional raid on a bird nest should be expected and serves the purpose of keeping bird populations in check. If you provide nest boxes, be sure to place them in spots that are not too vulnerable to predation.

A bird feeder can be mounted on a pole that has a baffle large enough to keep raccoons from climbing up and around it. Alternatively, you can bring the feeder in at night, when raccoons are most active. Occasionally, one of these animals may venture out during the day if it is hungry and does not feel threatened, but raccoons are normally nocturnal.

If you have a compost pile, all your plant wastes—material from the garden as well as fruit and vegetable scraps from the kitchen—should be added to it. Most vegetative scraps that result from meal preparation (rinds, onion skins, seeds, and so on) are not attractive to wild mammals. However, bones and fat removed from meat should never be put into a compost pile, because raccoons and other wildlife will definitely be attracted to the odors that develop. Although you should not mind them eating an occasional snack at your compost pile, you do not want to encourage the habit.

To prevent raccoons from tipping over the garbage can and making a mess, you need to minimize the rotting odors that emanate from the can. You can do this by wrapping any meat scraps in a zip-style plastic bag, preferably one that has already been used for some other purpose. For instance, I use zip-top bags to keep cereal fresh in my pantry and to help protect it from ants. When the cereal is gone, I save the bag to use later when I have meat scraps to dispose of.

However, this may not be enough to keep animals with a keen sense of smell out of the garbage can. You may need to buy cans that have snap-locking handles. And if you can keep the cans in a shed or garage, even better.

The Virginia Opossum is usually not much of a problem for people. These nocturnal scavengers feed mostly on dead animals—think of them as nature's sanitation workers. Numerous opossums end up as roadkill, hit by vehicles while eating animals that already met the same fate. Virginia Opossums also feed on small mammals, birds, snakes, frogs, and insects, as well as other invertebrates and fruits. A properly fenced garden will keep opossums out. They may get into an occasional bird's nest, so be careful in the placement of your nest boxes. Virginia Opossums may themselves make use of a bird box if it is big enough (for example, a screech owl box), because they are both terrestrial and arboreal. If an opossum decides to

Bird boxes should really be called wildlife boxes. Any kind of animal that makes use of natural cavities in dead trees might move into a box put up for birds.

sleep or nest in one of your boxes, take advantage of this rather rare opportunity to view a live opossum!

Black Bears

The American Black Bear is a large, extremely strong animal that cannot be excluded from the garden by any means other than electric fencing. However, few crops are attractive to these animals, so you may completely avoid bear problems in the garden if you refrain from growing sweet corn, apples, and certain other crops. If you live in bear country and you want to maintain your own beehives or raise chickens, you will need to do so in an enclosed area protected by electricity.

Bears, like raccoons, are scavengers that perform the important service of cleaning up dead animals. They also limit animal and plant reproduction by feeding upon animals young and old as well as various seeds and plants.

The same tricks employed for keeping raccoons out of the garbage may work for bears as well. If a bear is able to figure out how to open locking handles or it is not deterred by bungee cords, buy a length of metal chain long enough to rope through the handles and over the lid of the can. Pull the chain tight, then connect the chain back on itself with a snap chain link. This method has worked well for me. Still, wild animals often have a difficult time finding food, and extreme hunger can lead them to take extreme measures to get to any food available, no matter where it is located. A bear motivated by hunger and able to smell rotting food inside a can is probably strong enough to get into almost anything. My neighbor built a cage out of two-by-fours and metal fencing to house his garbage cans, which has worked successfully for many years. When people are more thoughtful and careful in their habits, they are able to avoid many conflicts with wildlife.

Bears may tear apart bird boxes if they are within easy reach on poles. This kind of activity is not common where I live, even though there are quite a few bears in my area. If your experience is different, the only solution is to remove the bird boxes altogether.

If you live in bear territory and feed birds, expect bears to get into your feeders. For many years I endured broken feeders following each bear visit, and I would have to stop feeding the birds for several days to give the bear time to move on. I was not pleased with this situation and implored my husband to come up with a way to discourage bears from getting to my feeders.

His solution was to plant a threaded galvanized pole in concrete so that the top of it was about nine and a half feet above the ground. Using galvanized threaded reducers, connectors, and pipe lengths, he fashioned four arms at the top of the pole from which to hang feeders. He then drilled a hook into the end of a wooden broom handle to extend my reach, allowing me to hang the feeders from the ground. My husband's new and improved bird feeder pole has been very successful, although a very large bear can make its way—albeit with difficulty—over the baffle, and a young bear can be tiresomely noisy as it tries to get around the baffle. Therefore, it is still sometimes necessary to chase a bear away (the American Black Bear is usually afraid of people, unless someone has "befriended" it—a very bad idea) and to bring in the feeders.

Bears are very strong and can easily tear apart feeders for seeds. The author's husband devised this bear-resistant feeder, which works extremely well.

Mice

There are numerous species of mice, and they are all extremely important in the food chain. Being near the bottom, mice provide food for many kinds of animals, and they need to produce young almost constantly to avoid being eliminated from the environment.

As consumers of seeds, mice will be attracted to your yard if you have bird feeders. To keep the mouse population inhabiting your area at a reasonable number, limit

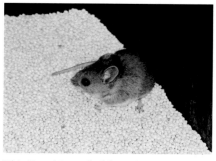

This Deer Mouse had feasted upon white millet in the author's shed after she forgot to replace the container's cover. Animals that carry seeds to their nests usually drop some of them along the way and therefore help to spread plants.

the amount of bird seed you put out each day. Inevitably, some seeds will be dropped on the ground, but there is nothing wrong with that. You are not trying to wipe out the mouse population—just limit it.

In addition, you should never leave pet food outside overnight. Proper sanitation around your home goes a long way toward avoiding problems with wild creatures. If you eliminate their food supplies, you will most likely force them to move on to better feeding grounds.

If mice get into your home or other structures on your property, try to locate the entrances they are using and plug them with caulk or quick-drying cement. For larger openings, one-quarter-inch hardware cloth is an effective barrier. If you cannot locate the holes the animals are using to gain entry, you may have no choice but to use spring-loaded traps to kill the mice that get inside. These traps are inexpensive, and more important, humane, usually killing the mouse instantly.

You should *never* use poison to control rodents. It causes suffering and a cruel death. In addition, dying rodents are easy prey for the many larger animals that eat them. These predators will also be sickened and die if they feed upon poisoned mice.

One winter, a beautiful Snowy Owl visited Virginia from the Far North. The large white raptor found its way to the Shenandoah Valley, where birders discovered it hanging around farms, with their plentiful supply of rodents. Seeing this magnificent creature was a treat for people who enjoy birds. Sadly, the owl was found dead one day. It was heartrending to look at its body and realize that the lovely white owl had traveled so many hundreds, perhaps thousands, of miles to try to survive the winter, only to die an unnatural and painful death in Virginia. An autopsy revealed its fate: death by rodent poisoning.

Coyotes

Coyotes have spread eastward and now inhabit areas throughout the United States. Because they are carnivores that feed on other animals, coyotes and people are often in conflict. Though they help to get deer and geese numbers under control, Coyotes will also eat cats and dogs, so owners need to take responsibility for the safety of their pets by keeping them inside or allowing them outside only with supervision.

Farmers who raise chickens should pen them every evening. Those who raise sheep or other domestic mammals should consider buying a llama. This South American ruminant has been employed quite successfully to guard sheep and other herd animals from predators.

Skunks, Moles, and Japanese Beetles

Beetle larvae, or grubs, constitute a large proportion of the diets of skunks and moles. A skunk finds grubs below ground level in lawns by digging down a few inches, creating a small pit. A mole employs its nose to locate grubs just under the soil surface and digs underground tunnels to get to these food morsels; the tunnels appear as ridges in a lawn or garden, usually becoming noticeable in spring or after a rain, when the soil is moist and therefore easier for a mole to dig through.

You should not get upset if you find skunk pits or mole tunnels. These signs indicate that you have grubs that, if allowed to become too numerous, may cause you and your plants more grief than the digging of a few animals. Without grub control, your plants could die, whereas the physical alterations wrought by these two mammals can be easily remedied. When you find little pits made by a skunk, simply replace the dirt that was dug out and piled right beside them. Mole tunnels can be easily tamped back down by walking on top of them.

Neither moles nor skunks will be numerous in any one area because they both have rather large home ranges. Depending on the species, there is typically only one skunk or mole per several acres; the animal will therefore be roaming over that entire area looking for food. Neither of these creatures will be in your vicinity for very long to feed. Moles, in particular, have such a high metabolism that they need to eat almost constantly, traveling over a wide area to find enough food to survive; a single Common (or Eastern) Mole usually inhabits over two acres. Therefore, buying traps or poison to eliminate these underground animals is completely uncalled for and a waste of money. A mole is continuously on the move and will not be in your yard for very long—unless, of course, you have an overpopulation of grubs, in which case you need its help.

Root-feeding beetle larvae can cause noticeable damage to lawns and other plants. After pupation (the process of metamorphosing into adults), the beetles may feed aboveground on flower blossoms and leaves. To control the beetle population, especially that of the Japanese Beetle, many people spread the spores of *Bacillus popilliae*, a natural disease bacterium of Japanese Beetles and their relatives, the Shining Leaf Chafers. The spores are mixed with talc to produce a dust and sold in bags labeled Milky Spore. The name is derived from the action of the spores upon the "blood" of infected grubs: it turns milky white.

Once Milky Spore is watered into the soil, the grubs eat it along with plant roots and other organic matter and are killed. Each dead grub serves as an incubator for billions of spores that are very resilient, surviving through freezing, flooding, and drought conditions. Although it may take three years to get a noticeable reduction in grub numbers, once the spores have become established, they probably remain permanently in your yard.

But Milky Spore, besides costing a lot in terms of your time and money, has costs to the environment as well. Milky Spore is a nonselective insecticide that can have serious consequences on your yard. Although it is often recommended as an "organic" control for the nonnative Japanese Beetle, it also kills close relatives of the Japanese Beetle that are native to our country. Thus, many of the beetles killed will be native species whose numbers may not need to be limited. Indeed, beetle grubs serve as vital food sources for other animals.

But more important, these insects are essential to your soil. Did you ever wonder how topsoil is created? Full of nutrients and completely friable, topsoil results from the activities of numerous organisms going about their business, literally under your feet. As beetle grubs feed upon organic matter in the soil (in addition to plant roots), they recycle it.

Keep in mind that because every organism's existence is tightly interwoven with that of numerous other organisms, and because every organism plays an important role in the proper workings of the environment, it is never wise to try to completely wipe out a population of any kind of native creature. Instead of buying Milky Spore, it would be far better to allow skunks and moles to serve as "natural insecticides." These animals do no serious harm to your yard while limiting the number of grubs to acceptable levels—saving your plants but still building soil. Consider yourself lucky if a skunk or a mole is dining on your property. In exchange for the minimal effort and time required to refill a few skunk holes or flatten a mole tunnel, you receive absolutely free, nontoxic grub control.

Voles and Snakes

An incredible number of gardeners have problems with voles (a type of meadow mouse). Voles are important in the environment because they help limit the number of plants in any one location. In the natural world, if plants kept reproducing without such controls, nature would have to use disease organisms to get rid of some of them. This is why plants (or animals) that are too crowded become diseased. But of course, a vole does not realize that it is not supposed to eat *your* plants.

There is only one surefire and safe way to limit the number of voles in your garden: allow snakes to coexist with you. Snakes are the only type of predator that can follow a vole down into its underground burrow. Without snakes, you are unlikely to be able to safely control the vole population on your property. Encourage snakes to live in your area by creating rock or log piles where they can take refuge during the heat of the day. Grow lots of flowers where they can hide from predators.

If you are afraid of being harmed by a snake, you can take a few simple precautions. *Always* watch where you are walking so that you do not step on a snake. It may react by trying to bite you—its only means of defense. If you are still nervous about stepping on a snake, wear leather boots. Then if a snake bites you, it will sink its teeth into the boot instead. You should wear leather gloves when gardening for the same reason.

The only kind of predator capable of following a vole down into its burrow is the snake. To prevent vole overpopulations, gardeners need to share their properties with reptiles such as this Black Rat Snake.

Another rule of thumb is to *never* stick your hands or feet into a place that is dark or otherwise obscured. You never know what might be in there. Use a long stick to gently poke among tall stalks to alert, without hurting, any animal that might be hiding there to your presence. Teach your children to do the same. When given the opportunity, animals will usually choose to flee rather than confront a human.

Aphids

Aphids are to songbirds (and ladybugs) as mice are to raptors and numerous mammals: a vital food source. Their abundance is a sure sign of their significance in the natural food chain, alerting us to the fact that many species feed upon them. Aphids must multiply rapidly in order to sustain their own numbers in the face of so much predation.

Although you may not care much about the numerous smaller animals that depend on aphids to survive, you probably care very much about resident and migratory birds. Songbirds are especially dependent upon the availability of aphids. So if you design your yard in a bird-

Healthy plants survive aphid feeding with the assistance of ladybug adults and larvae, which keep aphid numbers at manageable levels.

friendly manner, you will never have to worry about aphids. Small, clinging birds—such as chickadees and titmice—will feed upon aphids on the undersides of leaves.

Flower stalks left standing throughout the cold months of the year will provide aphids for insect-eating birds that may be visiting for the winter or passing through to areas farther south.

In a wildlife-friendly yard, aphids can be found on almost every kind of plant. They will not harm plants unless they become too numerous, a situation unlikely to occur if you live in agreement with nature.

Caterpillars and Bt

The spores of *Bacillus thuringiensis* (Bt), a bacterium, are commonly spread on crops to kill caterpillars. Touted by many sellers and authorities as an organic pesticide that is "harmless" to humans and other mammals, fish, birds, beneficial insect predators, and insect parasites, Bt seems like the perfect insecticide, but it is neither perfect nor harmless.

Most folks have no idea that numerous species of caterpillars can be killed by Bt. Formulated as either a dust that can be shaken over plants or a wettable powder that can be sprayed, this microbial pesticide can be carried to numerous other plants (there are thirty billion viable spores in approved formulations) if it is applied on a windy day. Any caterpillar that is feeding upon affected foliage will ingest the spores and die from intestinal paralysis within twenty-four to forty-eight hours. Therefore, nonproblematic caterpillars could be killed inadvertently.

Although Bt is not toxic to many animals, it can impact their lives indirectly. For example, caterpillars are a crucial dietary component for young birds, especially the migratory species whose numbers are in serious decline. Therefore, the removal of caterpillars from the environment can impair birds' ability to reproduce.

In addition, moth and butterfly populations are impacted directly by the deaths of caterpillars, reducing their own numbers and their ability to serve as a food source for the multitude of species that feed upon these winged adults. Bats, spiders, insects (such as the praying mantis), and night-flying birds (nighthawks, owls, Whip-poor-wills) all feed on moths and butterflies.

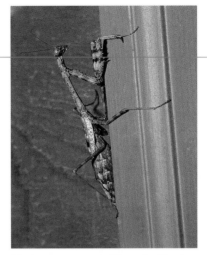

Unless you are a farmer with many acres of crops, you should not need to use Bt. If you visit your garden every day and check your plants carefully, you should be able to find caterpillars when they are still small and can be easily removed if there is an overabundance of them. If a plant still has many leaves and is thus not being seriously impacted, leave the caterpillars alone. Plants have coevolved with insects and can easily withstand a bit of feeding. Because caterpillars of most species typically feed for only

The large green mantids so familiar to people are nonnative and may be causing a decrease in the numbers of native Carolina Mantids like this one. Mantids are patient hunters that remain motionless, waiting for prey to land nearby.

about two weeks and a generation may be produced only once each year, your plants will have plenty of time to recover, suffering no lasting damage. You can monitor the feeding and do something about it when and if it really seems necessary. If you must take action, collect the caterpillars in a container and transfer them to your bird feeding area. The birds will be delighted with the easy pickings. Or, if you have a pond, you can drop the caterpillars into the water. (This mimics a natural occurrence, as caterpillars feeding on nearby plants sometimes fall into the water.) The wildlife in the pond (newts, frogs, tadpoles, water striders) and even goldfish will enjoy the tasty meal.

If you have encouraged wildlife around your home, even handpicking caterpillars should be unnecessary; predators or parasites should find most of them before they reach adulthood. Remember, however, that every organism has an important role to play in the environment, so you should not expect every caterpillar to be eaten.

To minimize the likelihood of your plantings being overwhelmed by any one kind of insect, interplant different species or varieties. By growing a few plants of various kinds together, you make it more difficult for a female insect to find the one kind of plant she needs to lay her eggs on.

It is also a good idea to grow numerous plants of the same kind around the yard so that the female has a choice of plants on which to lay her eggs. Insects do not want to doom their young to death by placing them where there will be insufficient food. If a plant already has eggs, a female will usually attempt to find another plant with few or no eggs.

You should avoid killing caterpillars unnecessarily, especially if you do not know what kind they are. The caterpillars on your flowers, shrubs, or trees, may be the larvae of beautiful moths and butterflies that will bring much pleasure when you see them flying around your yard.

Black Widow Spiders are shy creatures that stick to dark spaces and are rarely seen by people. Chances are slim you will ever be bitten as long as you keep your hands and feet out of places that you can not see into very well.

Venomous Spiders

I have often been told by folks in my home state that they have killed Brown Recluse Spiders. Yet the venomous Brown Recluse is a western arachnid that does not live in Virginia. It saddens me that spiders are being killed unnecessarily because people have misidentified them. It is also a shame that people assign such a high probability of harm to a creature that is highly unlikely to be encountered at all. And even if it is, the probability of harm is minuscule if people would use common sense and take a few precautions.

The Brown Recluse and the Black Widow, another venomous spider, are both arachnids of dark, out-of-the-way places. Neither species is aggressive, preferring to escape rather than to deal with human beings. If you live where these spiders exist, never blindly stick your hands or feet into dark places. Outside, do not lay down towels or clothing where a spider might be hiding, such as in a woodpile or among a jumble of rocks. Teach children how to avoid these spiders as well.

Because most people know little or nothing about venomous spiders, they are fearful, and as a result, these spiders (or any spider that might be mistaken for them) are killed unnecessarily. Unfamiliarity creates irrational fear. Learn about wildlife so that you can coexist with these creatures, even if it means that you need to practice reasonable caution.

Bagworms

When people talk about bagworms, they are referring to the larvae of the bagworm moth. There are many species, but the one most commonly encountered is the Evergreen Bagworm moth.

The caterpillar of a bagworm moth encases itself in a portable silken case (the "bag") that is covered with bits of debris, such as leaves, twigs, or dried evergreen needles. As the caterpillar grows, it enlarges its case. When it is ready to transform into the adult form, it attaches the case to a twig with silk and pupates within it.

The Evergreen Bagworm feeds mostly on cedars (junipers). Because so many varieties of these plants are available at nurseries, whole neighborhoods may be extensively landscaped with evergreens that attract bagworm moths. In a yard that is landscaped with wildlife in mind, however, bagworms are seldom a problem. Despite the many native Eastern Red Cedars around my house, I see only one bagworm a year, if that—and it is never even on a cedar. I always find it attached to the window in my cellar door.

I actually find the spindle-shaped case of the bagworm quite interesting. Because it is covered with dried cedar needles, it looks like it belongs on a tree. If one of my trees ever had a large number of these insects, I would probably just think of it as being covered with a type of cone, as on pine trees.

If you have trees that are overwhelmed by bagworms, your yard is not functioning properly and is devoid of the predators that prey upon bagworms. This situation is often the result of using pesticides that kill numerous species of insects, including the bagworm's insect predators. Or you may need to revamp your landscape to encourage more insect-eating birds to nest nearby. Some birds are quite adept at recognizing insect camouflage tactics (such as the very natural-looking bag), and other birds know how to look under leaves to ferret out the adult moths. Lizards, salamanders, and small mammals also hunt for insects and keep their populations down. However, only a healthy yard supports these inhabitants.

If you have only a few bags hanging on your trees, resist the urge to use pesticides. Just handpick or clip the bags off of the trees.

Bluebirds and Blowflies

In all of my decades of cleaning bird boxes, I have never yet found a nest that was obviously full of parasites. If you find an overabundance of parasites in a nest box, something is out of kilter. Perhaps the main reason for an overpopulation of these creatures is a lack of sanitation on the part of the humans maintaining the box.

Blowfly larvae are considered a threat to bluebirds in particular, although they also feed upon Tree, Barn, and Cliff Swallows, House Wrens, and American Robins, among others. Female blowflies lay their eggs on newly hatched nestlings. After the eggs hatch, the blowfly larvae suck the blood of the young birds during the night. At daybreak, the larvae go down to the nest bottom, where they cannot be seen by the adult birds tending their young.

In areas devoid of dead trees where bluebirds can nest, these beautiful birds will reuse the same box many times over, building a new nest right on top of an old one. But in the wild, if nest sites are plentiful, birds tend to move on to a new site after their young have fledged; this helps limit parasite populations. If the numbers of flies, lice, mites, and other animals that suck the blood from bird nestlings and adults became too high, the parasites would kill their food source. Eventually, there might be no more birds to feed upon, dooming future generations of the parasites.

Indeed, because birds have coevolved with blowflies, healthy nestlings can withstand a few parasites. However, if you want to minimize the number of blowfly larvae in a nest box, be sure to clean the box after the young have fledged. Remove the nest and sweep out any debris on the floor of the box. However, do not destroy the nest by burning it or tearing it apart. The nest may contain tiny (less than one-sixteenth of an inch) chalcid wasp larvae, one of the natural predators of blowflies. Place the nest on the ground in a somewhat protected area where it will not get soaked by rain.

Many people also use blowfly traps, made from a piece of hardware cloth. The trap takes up the entire floor of the box, but the ends are bent so that the trap sits about one inch off of the floor. The legless blowfly larvae fall through the trap holes, cannot climb back up to the nest to feed upon the bluebird nestlings, and starve at the bottom of the box.

To manage your box in the most humane manner for both bird and blowfly, simply remove each nest as soon as the young have fledged.

A Cautionary Note

Many people worry about catching diseases from wildlife. However, if you never touch wild animals, you are unlikely to catch an illness. It is also a good idea to wear a nose mask to avoid breathing in debris when cleaning out bird boxes or anyplace an animal has nested.

People usually get into trouble when they handle wildlife and get bitten. A friend of mine once found an entire brood of baby bats and could not resist the urge to handle the small, delicate creatures. One little bat bit him, and even though the bite did not draw blood, he had to go through the trouble and expense of getting rabies shots. Because the rabies virus is deadly and not treatable after symptoms develop, he had no choice but to be safe rather than sorry. I am delighted to say that the local health department did not insist—as it would have in an earlier, unenlightened time—that all of the baby bats be killed. Bats provide extremely effective insect control, so killing them unnecessarily is uncalled for and unwise.

Many people fear bats, but a friend of the author decided to handle some young Evening Bats he found in his house. Not surprisingly, he got nipped and had to get rabies shots to be safe.

Unfortunately, people receive an endorsement to touch wild animals when museum staff, park naturalists, and other professionals allow the public (especially children) to handle wildlife under their direction. Often these animals are disabled and can no longer survive in the wild.

Many nature centers sell food to customers so they can feed the animals, giving people the idea that wild animals can be treated as "pets in the making."

Yellow-bellied Sapsucker holes are not detrimental to trees and shrubs. This extremely large and old Common Hackberry tree is covered with hundreds of sapsucker wells.

However, such presentations send a mixed message to both children and adults, leaving the impression that wild animals are pets in the making.

Instead, people should be taught that all wildlife should be watched and not touched. We love to connect emotionally and physically to other species, but in most cases, we should not do so—for their sake and ours.

When you understand the natural world, you no longer see wildlife as pests that need to be eliminated but rather as helpers that need to be encouraged. You view the natural world as a fascinating place that is full of surprises and endless possibilities. You accept the natural look of plants, not worrying about spotted leaves or tiny holes. Healthful gardening practices are more important to you than artificial perfection. Wildlife gardeners accept the natural world on its own terms, and they are more contented as a result.

Chapter 10

Accessible Gardening

Whether from increasing age, accident, disease, or a congenital physical disability, many of us must learn to deal with limited mobility. I was diagnosed with rheumatoid arthritis almost two decades ago, and my everyday activities quickly became excruciatingly painful to perform. There were days when I would go outside to garden and find that the pain in my hands was just too great. I would return to the house in tears because I could no longer do what I had always loved.

I decided early on not to give up; I was determined to continue doing the things I enjoyed. This chapter is meant to help people in similar circumstances to continue or even begin to garden in agreement with nature. But it can also help those who are fortunate enough to be healthy and completely mobile. It contains information and practical advice for gardening more easily and more safely, no matter what your physical condition. But first, I want to emphasize that a garden that teems with wildlife is a garden

A garden that welcomes wildlife is a garden that is full of surprises for the astute gardener. Many life-forms, such as this Clymene Moth, sport spectacular designs or coloration.

that keeps our minds from dwelling on negative thoughts, provides peace of mind, and encourages an overall sense of well-being.

Embracing a New Gardening Philosophy

Studies have shown that gardening is an uplifting pursuit. To gardeners, this is not news. Anyone who has successfully nurtured plants—whether one potted houseplant or rows and rows of crops—has experienced firsthand how rewarding this activity can be.

But in order to enjoy gardening, you have to accept your limitations and work within them. I can attest to the fact that it is not always easy to confine yourself to realistic goals, but it is extremely important that you do not overextend yourself. Gardening requires the expenditure of energy, and if you try to do too much, gardening will become exhausting instead of enjoyable.

Although it is tempting to try to grow lots of different kinds of beautiful plants (especially once those irresistible garden catalogs begin to arrive in the mail), you should start small. If you find that you can do more than you originally thought, you can always spend more time in the yard and add more plants.

Two very important mental changes will allow you to garden more easily and happily: altering your idea of what constitutes a lovely landscape and revamping your opinion of garden maintenance as work. Rethinking what kind of landscape is aesthetically acceptable can make a big difference in how much effort it takes to maintain your property. For instance, if you own many acres, it will be much easier on you (and the environment) to allow some of that acreage to exist in a natural state with wild grasses and flowers. (Please note, however, that it will need to be cut—in late winter or very early spring—every second or third year. This timing prevents trees from becoming the dominant species and allows wildlife to make use of food plants all fall and well into the winter.)

Also, you should allow yourself to be less biased and more tolerant of certain plants that have undeserved bad reputations. For example, what is wrong with the Common Dandelion? This little flower is one of my favorite plants. Dandelions are one of the first flowers to bloom in the spring. With their bright, cheerful yellow blooms, they can lift us out of the winter doldrums—but only if we let them!

Perhaps even more important than lifting our spirits, these blossoms supply much-needed nectar (and pollen) to the first insects that rouse on warm late-winter and early-spring days. In fall, they perform this critically important function for late-migrating Monarch butterflies when few—if any—other plants are blooming. This sustenance helps these creatures make their way to Mexico. How can anyone disparage a plant that plays such an important role in the lives of the beautiful Monarchs?

Would you like to see a patch of bright yellow dandelions taking to the air? American Goldfinches love the seeds of Common Dandelions and will flock to them in spring and summer. When the male birds fly off together, their bright yellow plumage perfectly matches the bright yellow of the dandelions, giving one the sensation that these flowers are magically flying away.

Dandelions are often the only flowers blooming in mid to late fall, when Monarchs are migrating along the eastern part of the country. Thus these lovely plants, so often despised by people, can be incredibly helpful to late-leaving butterflies, which need all of the help they can get.

Additionally, you should try to envision the effort required to maintain your yard as healthful exercise instead of unpleasant work. When you embrace this way of thinking, gardening can become a pleasurable and even exciting experience. For example, consider the removal of unwanted plants (which I prefer to call "volunteers" rather than "weeds" because of the latter's bad connotation). Most folks detest this activity, but I find it enjoyable because I never know what might happen. When I get down close to the ground, I observe animals that I probably would not have seen otherwise.

One day while I was pulling out plants in one of my garden beds, I uncovered a smallish snake that looked like an oversized earthworm. When I looked it up in my field guide, I was amused to find that the little serpent is actually called a Worm Snake and that its main food is earthworms. Because Worm Snakes usually slither around at night and hide during the day, they are not often seen by people.

On yet another day, as I was bent down in my strawberry patch, I heard a rustling sound behind me. As I slowly stood up and turned around, I noticed some strawberry plants moving several feet away from me. But when I began to make my way toward that area, the movement stopped and I saw nothing. I went back to my original spot, and within a few moments, I heard the rustling again. This time, I moved ever so carefully toward the moving strawberry plants and spotted a Northern Short-tailed Shrew, presumably searching for a meal of arthropods. Because these shrews prefer to tunnel under leaf litter, they are seldom seen by humans. This particular animal was content to "tunnel" under strawberry leaves still on the plants, and since I was gardening nearby, I was privileged to get a few glimpses of it going about its everyday activities.

So think of weeding as a very slow nature walk. Just this little adjustment in the way you think will reward you with many delightful moments. Gardening with the right philosophy not only makes gardening more enjoyable, it makes life more enjoyable!

Gardening Healthfully and Safely

It is especially important to perform gardening tasks with proper body mechanics, which simply means moving your body carefully and correctly to avoid undue stress. It is also crucial to keep your muscles strong and your joints limber. The older you are, the more important this advice is. As your body ages, it is actually wearing out (as unpleasant as this is to admit). Therefore, the older you are, the easier it is to injure yourself. Worse yet, mending an injury is also much more difficult and occurs more slowly than when you were younger. So it is best to avoid injuries in the first place.

If you are not already an ardent exerciser or you have concerns about whether it is reasonable to engage in a particular activity, consult your doctor and ask for a referral to a physical or occupational therapist. These exercise experts can help you to tailor an exercise program that works for you, from the proper way to stretch muscles to the least stressful way to use your joints.

Before doing any strenuous work or exercise, always do some stretching to loosen tight muscles. Tight muscles are more easily torn and can cause joint injury.

Walking is a great overall exercise that is good for your entire body, which will assist your gardening efforts. This activity can be performed almost anywhere, and the only expense involved is a good pair of walking shoes. Certified pedorthists on staff at some sports-shoe stores can give you advice on the best shoes for your gait.

When planning the location of your garden, consider which spot will be easiest to take care of. For example, be sure that your garden is sited near a source of water. Carrying hoses or watering cans any appreciable distance can be fatiguing. If you can locate the garden near a tool or storage shed, you can eliminate a lot of walking to retrieve forgotten tools. Alternatively, place a weatherproof chest or large box right inside the garden to keep your tools handy. Small tools (such as hand cultivators or trowels) can also be stored in a garden tool pouch or apron or in a wheeled cart or wheelbarrow that you can bring to the garden with you.

To avoid the effort involved in growing plants from seeds, consider buying transplants from nurseries or garden catalogs. This option is more expensive and may restrict your choice of varieties, but it is much less expensive in terms of energy expended. Be sure to pick plants that do not require a lot of care; for example, choose drought-tolerant plants if you live in an arid area where rain showers would not provide sufficient water. And to really lessen the work from year to year, be sure to choose some perennial plants so that you will not have to replant the entire garden every year.

Always garden during the time of day when you feel the most ambitious and capable of performing the tasks at hand, whether that is first thing in the morning or later in the afternoon. People with rheumatoid arthritis are often plagued by morning stiffness in their fingers, so it may take a few hours before they can garden without severe pain.

Always pace yourself and alternate activities. Do not move too quickly, and do not stay in the same position or perform the same activity (such as pruning or pulling plants) for prolonged periods. Let your body be your guide. If you feel like you are running out of energy, take a break; sit down and enjoy the fresh air and wildlife around you. A wonderful idea is to locate a garden bench or a picnic table with benches close to the garden to provide an inviting place to relax. You can take advantage of this opportunity to rehydrate yourself with a glass of water. If you feel up to gardening again after fifteen to twenty minutes, switch to a new task that will work a different part of your body. But if you are still tired or in pain, call it a day. If you have sore or painful muscles or joints twenty-four hours after gardening, try to figure out how you overdid it and limit yourself the next time.

Alternate hands to avoid strain. Whenever you have to grasp an item, such as a hoe, rake, shovel, or trowel, you are utilizing muscles that can be hurt if they are employed for too long. To avoid an overuse injury, alternate between your left and right hands to hold the tool. Although it will undoubtedly feel awkward at first to use your nondominant hand, it gets easier over time: practice makes perfect. Also, purchase garden tools that have padded or otherwise enlarged handles to make them easier to grasp. The less tightly you have to close your fingers, the less strain you create on the joints and muscles in your hands.

One of the easiest ways to get hurt is to bend over from the waist, placing a great deal of strain on the spinal column and lower back muscles. Twisting your back has the same effect. Instead of bending from the waist, bend your knees to get down to a lower level when picking up or putting down something. This utilizes your thigh muscles, which are less apt than your back to be seriously strained. To lift a heavy object, squat down, pull the object close, tighten your stomach muscles, and stand up. If you must turn to put the object where you want it, turn your feet and then deposit the object where it needs to go; do not twist your back. Also, hold the object close to your body at waist level. If you hold a weight away from your body, it will pull your spine forward, straining your back as it tries to compensate to keep you on your feet.

To avoid bending over to plant seeds, purchase or make (or have someone else make) raised planters that are at a comfortable height for you to work at while seated. Large, deep planter boxes, tubs, or whiskey half-barrels are good choices and readily available. If you make your own containers, resist the temptation to use treated lumber. Treated wood lasts longer, but it may leach harmful chemicals into the soil,

To avoid seriously injuring your back, avoid bending over from your waist when gardening (or doing anything else). Bending your knees allows you to use your thigh muscles instead of your lower back muscles, which can be easily hurt.

which is not good for people, pets, or wildlife. If the roots of food plants absorb such substances, the chemicals may be carried into the fruits or vegetables, which means that these chemicals could be ingested.

To avoid bending while picking vine fruits (such as cucumbers), grow them on a trellis. Trellises can also be absolutely gorgeous when planted with flowering vines (such as morning glories) that attract hummingbirds, moths, butterflies, and other insects. I love these "vertical gardens."

If you are like I am and also find squatting and kneeling to be hard on the body, you can sit on the ground when planting seeds or pulling plants or perhaps buy a padded garden kneeler. This device provides a soft surface to kneel on and is thus much easier on the knees. Some kinds of kneelers are reversible; when you turn it over, it becomes a convenient bench.

Many gardening catalogs also sell low-to-the-ground wheeled scooters that have swiveling tractor-style seats and oversized wheels to easily traverse grass and other soft surfaces (make sure the wheels are self-locking). Attached storage bags are sometimes an added bonus. These kinds of items can be rather expensive, but if they allow you to garden, they may be well worth the cost.

Always try to push instead of pull. Pushing allows you to use the larger, stronger muscles in your legs instead of the smaller muscles in your arms. And remember to keep your arms close to your sides instead of stretched out in front of you when digging, mowing, or raking. Extending your arms increases the likelihood that you will lean forward excessively, placing a strain on your lower back.

Purchasing tools (such as hoes and rakes) that have long handles will help you avoid bending too much and hurting your back. Also, keep your tools in tiptop shape to make using them less tiring. For example, pruners should be sharp and lubricated so that you do not have to force the blades through a stem.

Purchase a good pair of leather gardening gloves that fit properly. I was once accused of not being a "real" gardener because I always wore gloves instead of sinking my hands into the dirt and savoring the experience. This comment gave me quite a chuckle, because at the time, I had already spent decades growing many of my own fruits and vegetables. I had no doubt that I was a *real* gardener, and in fact, I considered myself to be a *smart* gardener to boot! There are good reasons to wear gloves when gardening, the least important of which is to keep your hands young looking and blemish free, not to mention clean. A more significant reason is to protect your hands from thorns, sharp stones, and the like. Leather gloves also serve as a barrier if you inadvertently touch a snake or a stinging or biting insect.

Despite these precautions, it is nearly impossible to work outside without eventually sustaining some type of minor cut or abrasion. Any break in the skin may allow bacteria to enter your body, and some bacteria can cause serious illness. Therefore, it is always a good idea to wash all wounds as soon as possible with soap and water (to flush the organisms away). Then, especially if you plan to continue working outside, cover the area with a bandage to protect the wound. I have never found it necessary to use antibiotic ointment. The human body can successfully fight off the effects of most bacteria. However, if you have a chronic illness that makes you more susceptible to infection, by all means apply some antibiotic to the affected area.

Anyone who plans to work outside should keep their tetanus shots up to date. Tetanus is an acute infectious disease caused by the toxin of a bacterium that usually enters the body through a wound. An early symptom is lockjaw, a spasm of the jaw muscles. A tetanus shot every ten years will protect you from contracting this disease.

When you pull out plants, try to do it when the ground is moist. An opportune time is a couple of days after a good rainfall, when plant roots can be more easily dislodged. However, avoid working in the garden when the soil is very wet, because walking around will compact the dirt.

Be sure to create wide paths throughout the entire garden so it is easy to get around. It takes more energy to fight your way through a tangle of plants or to walk a long way around plants to get to where you want to go. At best, this can be annoying; at worst, it can be quite tiring, thus shortening your gardening day.

If you live in an apartment with a balcony, or if maintaining a large garden is simply beyond your capabilities, you can still experience the joys of gardening with hanging pots of plants. To avoid having to climb up on something to water your hanging plants, try using a wand extension that attaches to your garden hose or kitchen sink. Or you can devise a pulley system: Hammer two nails vertically (one placed above the other) on a wall near the plant. Attach a pulley to a support timber in the ceiling or overhang. Tie a rope to the pot hanger and thread it through the pulley to pull the potted plant up into the air. Tie the other end of the rope around the two nails in a figure-eight pattern. To lower the plant back down for fertilizing, watering, or pruning, just undo the figure eight. If you use small, lightweight pots for hanging baskets, you might be able to just use a broom handle with a hook drilled into the end to snag the hanging pots.

Use lightweight planters on your balcony, deck, or porch. A lightweight planter is easier to move into the desired location. Try to arrange the planters in their permanent positions before filling them with soil and plants to avoid moving heavy pots. If you must move a filled pot, do so when the soil is dry, just before watering.

No matter what kind of gardening you do, there may be tasks that are better left for others to perform. There is no shame in admitting that you are not up to a particular task and asking or paying for help. If someone's assistance allows you to continue to enjoy the beauty of your garden, it is well worth it.

It is important to recognize that, over time, you may be unable to garden like you used to. This is unfortunate, but the sooner you accept and adjust to your limitations, the happier you will be. For example, after decades of tending to a 2,000-square-foot garden and then canning and preserving the fruits of my labors to enjoy throughout the winter, I had to face the fact that these tasks demanded more energy than I could afford to expend. It was several years before I could bring myself to give away my beloved canning supplies, but once I did, I found it much easier to move on.

I investigated other means of preserving food and discovered, much to my delight, that in some cases freezing worked just as well—or even better. I even found a recipe for freezer pickles that were better than the canned ones I made for years. And the preparation is a whole lot easier.

I started to cultivate only as much of my fenced garden as I could take care of, and I allowed the lower portion of the garden to become a wildflower meadow. None of the plants were placed there by me; they are all volunteers. By July, that section of the garden is a riot of color, the result of hundreds of variously hued blooms and numerous species of butterflies and other insects flitting from blossom to blossom. It is a bounty of beauty that does not cost me money, time, or effort. Instead of

Day-flying Snowberry Clearwing Moths resemble bumblebees and are sometimes confused with them.

gathering food, I harvest the sheer pleasure that is there for the taking—and sharing: visitors marvel at the sight!

The lower part of the garden also serves as a "laboratory" of sorts, where I can discover new kinds of wildlife and add to my knowledge of the natural world. In a very real sense, the meadow functions as an outdoor entertainment center, health spa, and school all in one, where I can listen to birds singing, breathe fresh air, and be enthralled by the revelations of nature.

It is not easy to alter your life. But if you learn acceptance, you may find new avenues that bring you more joy than you ever could have imagined.

Chapter 11

The Healing Garden

In late 1992, my mother was diagnosed with terminal cancer, and I brought her to my home to care for her. Within a few months, she became bedridden and I had to provide for her every need, twenty-four hours a day.

Although the next year was physically exhausting, the emotional aspect of dealing with her impending death was even tougher. I dared not cry in front of my mother, because she was the type of person who always maintained a stiff upper lip. However, I had to allow my tears to flow at some point each day, which I did down by my pond, safely out of sight and earshot of my ailing mother.

When I visited the pond during the spring, summer, and early fall of 1993, I would find the bees working hard, flying from blossom to blossom to gather nectar or pollen for

A bee feeds at Obedient Plant, whose name comes from the bloom's ability to stay put if turned away from its usual position.

The White-tailed Dragonfly is a common visitor to ponds. This particular one kept the author company when she visited her pond during her mother's fatal illness.

their colonies. Butterflies flitted from plant to plant to obtain each flower's sweet liquid, oblivious of the beauty they lent to the environment with their colorful wings. Dragonflies, perched on dried flower stalks from the previous summer, watched for flying insects that they could grab for a meal.

Within the pond, I would see—through eyes brimming with tears— my goldfish waiting for me to throw them some fish flakes. Eastern Newts swam lazily just under the surface of the water, as if they did not have a care in the world. The resident Green Frogs eventually became bold enough to remain sitting on the rocks across the pond from me instead of jumping into the water at my approach. Birds sometimes flew in quite close to get a drink of water, as if they did not realize that I was alive.

Watching all these creatures, I would find the strength to return to the house with a big smile for my mother. The wildlife at the pond was so *alive* and so full of purpose that their exuberance rubbed off on me and helped me pull myself together and get through the rest of the day. As a result, I was able to make the most of the time my mom and I had left together.

After my mother died, I wondered why I had been drawn to the pond and why it had been able to help me deal with my grief. I concluded that the life in and around my pond had helped me reconnect to the outside world. My personal world inside the house had been falling apart, but the external world—as demonstrated by all of the life-forms down by the pond—had continued on, as if nothing of great impact was happening. It was obvious that the world (life) does indeed go on, even though you might carry the pain of a loved one's death for the rest of your days.

In 1993 I had never heard of a "healing garden." Having been interested in nature since childhood, I had always had a garden wherever I lived. But in 1993, I discovered the true power of nature when my pond and all the organisms associated with it gave me the strength to make it through that heartbreaking year. It was not until May 2000 that I became aware of the concept of a healing garden. About ten years earlier, some keenly insightful people had realized that we all might be physically and psychologically healthier if nature were a part of our lives.

The National Federation of Garden Clubs is one group that has taken this idea to heart. Its members are making an effort to add gardens to hospitals, nursing homes, adult day-care centers, hospices, and assisted-living complexes for the benefit of residents and visitors alike. It is not surprising that garden clubs would take an interest in creating healing gardens, since gardeners love to garden. What is more significant is that gardeners are intuitively aware of how restorative the natural world can be to a person's state of mind. A gardener just understands the value of a garden.

How can nature be such an important component of our health and well-being? Undoubtedly, the answer lies in the fact that we are very much a part of the natural world, even though many folks seem to be quite removed from it. Living in cities of concrete and steel or towns paved over with asphalt, it might seem as if contact with nature is nonessential. But even the largest cities have parks (for example, Central Park in New York City), and our federally preserved natural areas (such as Yellowstone National Park) are overcrowded with tourists every summer. There can be no denying that humans feel a need to connect with nature, even if the natural world is not a part of their daily lives.

Scientific studies are not required to prove the downright necessity of interacting with nature—at least on some level. However, such studies have shown that nature can have a powerful role in the physical healing process, especially in tension-filled environments such as hospitals. Researchers have found that hospital patients who looked out on a natural setting recovered more quickly than those who looked out on a brick wall. The theory is that a patient who is able to view trees and flowers experiences a reduction of stress, inducing a sense of well-being that promotes health.

There are now horticultural therapists who use plants to relieve stress and to improve patients' moods. Additionally, therapists have found that the simple, repetitive motions involved in gardening can serve as a form of physical therapy for severely traumatized patients.

Families of patients in health care facilities can also benefit from a garden on the property. A garden provides a tranquil site where both patients and their families can find respite from the overwhelming atmosphere of sickness and the sense of loss of control over one's life that accompanies illness. With plants growing all around and wildlife busily going about its business, one's mind is distracted from oneself and is caught up in another reality. A garden allows release from the prison that is the human body.

I have experienced the restorative power of nature, so I know first-hand the value of gardens, especially those that contain wildlife as well as plants. Therefore, I want to encourage you to get involved in beginning, restoring, or maintaining a garden around your home or someone else's home; around schools, parks, libraries, and businesses; and especially in health care settings. I encourage you to use this book to help create gardens of native and naturalized plants that will not demand a lot of care.

And do not overlook the value of bird feeders in a healing garden, especially in urban areas—even if House Sparrows, Rock Pigeons, and European Starlings are the only birds to attract. Feeding these nonnative birds may be frowned upon by many nature enthusiasts, but it can make all the difference to a lonely or ill person living in a city, where most native birds find it impossible to survive.

Before her final illness, my mom lived alone in a ground-floor apartment on the outskirts of a city. (Although any of her children would have taken her in, my mother worried that she would be a burden to us.) When I would call every week, she would tell me about "her" birds. Renters at the apartment complex were not allowed to own pets or to feed birds, but my mother—undoubtedly feeling a need for companionship—would put birdseed and water under her window air conditioner, which was hidden from view by a large evergreen shrub. Although she could not actually see the House Sparrows that somehow managed to discover the food and came to eat, Mom could hear their twittering. Just listening to their "conversations" gave my mother a lift that—I am sure—eased her loneliness. And taking care of those birds, especially in the severe cold and snow of the Massachusetts winter, no doubt allowed my mother to feel useful and needed in this world.

I believe that people could experience more happiness, better health, a sense of peace, and far less stress if everyone had a healing garden to help them through the day. When you possess your own personal sanctuary that supports other creatures, it is easier to come to terms with the painful and unavoidable difficulties of life.

I am quite confident that my mom's hidden—and, sadly, forbidden—sanctuary kept her alive far longer than if she had had to endure hours of silence in between chats with her far-flung offspring. That one tall evergreen shrub provided her with the tiniest of healing gardens. Yet it provided a sanctuary big enough to fill my mother's living room with the life-affirming chattering of "her" birds.

A healing garden does not have to be large to be effective, especially if it supports wildlife.

FINAL THOUGHTS

If I could have one wish, I would wish for people to understand the value of gardening with wildlife in mind. Society as a whole would then embrace this concept. Yards would contain very little lawn. People would grow shrubs and trees and numerous flowers, with brush piles tucked in here and there. Birds would be singing everywhere! Shops on small lots in towns would grow potted plants to attract butterflies to their doorways. Larger businesses with more land would create wildlife meadows with paths for employees, customers, and neighbors to walk on. There would be no need for pesticides, so our waterways would be purer and better able to support aquatic life. There would be less need for mowing, meaning cleaner air and less noise pollution. The environment would function as it was meant to function, allowing people to sit back, relax, and enjoy their yards.

If you would love to live in the environment I just described—and that I believe is possible to create—then I hope you will expand your personal efforts to your community.

Even a small yard such as this one in Mt. Olive, Virginia, can be made wildlife-friendly by minimizing lawn and growing lots of flowers, shrubs, and trees.

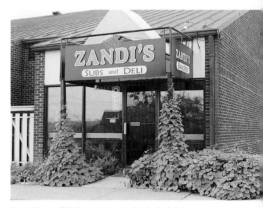

Retail establishments can be helpful to local wildlife and people by growing flowers around their businesses, as seen here in Charlottesville, Virginia.

The tall sunflower in front of this barbershop in Waynesboro, Virginia, helps to make it a wildlife- and people-friendly location.

With less grass to mow and maintain, our air and waterways would be much cleaner and healthier for people and wildlife. Moorman's River in Sugar Hollow, Virginia, is a scenic river that is jealously guarded by adjacent property owners who care about wildlife and their own health. Some folks grow no grass at all, maintaining forest in its natural state around their houses.

In addition to implementing this vision in your own yard, talk to other folks about the importance of living in agreement with nature. Explain to anyone who will listen how much we need wildlife and how enjoyable it is to live in wildlife habitat instead of in the sterile, unnatural human environments that are currently so prevalent. Encourage local and state government leaders to alter "weed ordinances" so that more natural landscaping becomes the standard. Suggest to government planners that more natural settings be created around government buildings, where less mowing also means less expense for taxpayers. And ask them to officially recognize home owners and businesses in the com-

This wonderfully land-scaped rest stop in Middletown, New York, is an example of how government prop-erties, no matter how big or small, can be managed for wildlife and people.

munity that participate in this effort. We all require a cleaner, healthier environment than the one we now live in.

If you are a bold soul who is not afraid of public speaking, address garden and other nature-related clubs about the ramifications of main-taining landscapes that consist mostly of lawn. Speak to leaders of the local business community about the value of making gardens that are attractive to human eyes as well as beneficial to wildlife. And the leaders of tomorrow are in elementary, middle, and high schools today, so do not forget to include them in your outreach efforts.

If you live near an airport, encourage those who run the facility to leave unused areas overgrown for wildlife. For many years, a small air-port in northern Virginia hosted Short-eared Owls and Northern Harri-ers every winter. These owls and large hawks fed on rodents among the

Children naturally love and care about wildlife. Grown-ups should, too.

The Henley family of Crozet, Virginia, practices nature-friendly farming. Numerous wildflowers and native shrubs and trees grow among the acres and acres of orchards, bringing in pollinators and numerous other forms of wildlife to keep the land functioning in an almost natural state.

tall grasses away from the buildings. But alas, someone decided that the untrimmed areas were too messy, so that was the end of a perfect place for these northern birds to spend the winter.

If there are farmers in your area, offer to give a presentation to their local Ruritan Club. Many people envision farms as landscapes that automatically provide wildlife habitat, but today's farmers are as caught up in "cleanliness" as are suburban home owners. Nowadays, farms typically reflect the characteristic artificial landscape that most people strive for, even though such landscapes are costly to maintain.

But teaching by preaching is probably not as effective as showing by hoeing. If you can volunteer to help plant and maintain a garden created with wildlife in mind, your work may inspire other folks. Often, libraries and schools possess enough land to create wildlife gardens that could serve as places for patrons and students to relax and learn.

Perhaps you could interest the local parks department in setting aside an area for a natural garden. Once you demonstrate how much easier such a garden is to maintain compared with a lawn, the parks department might decide to enlarge the original garden. Bigger is better when you are landscaping for wildlife.

Finally, offer to plant and perhaps maintain a wildlife garden at a health care facility. People in nursing homes, hospices, and hospitals could benefit immeasurably from having a real garden nearby, complete with wildlife.

We need landscaping for wildlife in every possible setting: private, public, industrial, and institutional. What is good for the health of wildlife is also good for the health of humans. That is the nature of the garden.

If society would stop demanding that most areas with plants be mowed, natural areas could exist along roadways in towns and cities.

Scientific Names of Species

Animals

Amphibians
Frog
    Green: *Rana clamitans*
    Pickerel: *Rana palustris*
    Wood: *Rana sylvatica*
Salamander: order Caudata
    Eft, Red (juvenile form of Red-spotted or Eastern Newt)
    Newt, Eastern (or Red-spotted): *Notophthalmus viridescens*
    Redback: *Plethodon cinereus*
Toad
    American: *Bufo americanus*
    Fowler's: *Bufo woodhousei*
Treefrog
    Gray: *Hyla chrysoscelis, Hyla versicolor*
    Spring Peeper: *Hyla crucifer*

Arachnids
Daddy-long-legs: many species in order Opiliones
Spider: many species in order Araneae
    Black Widow: *Latrodectus mactans*
    Brown Recluse (or Violin): *Loxosceles reclusa*
    Crab: family Thomisidae
    Orb: family Araneidae
    Trapdoor: family Ctenizidae
    Wolf: family Lycosidae
    Violin: (see Brown Recluse)

Bacteria

Bt: *Bacillus thuringiensis*
Milky Spore: *Bacillus popilliae*
Tetanus: *Clostridium tetani*

Birds

Blackbird, Red-winged: *Agelaius phoeniceus*
Bluebird
    Eastern: *Sialia sialis*
    Mountain: *Sialia currucoides*
    Western: *Sialia mexicana*
Bunting
    Indigo: *Passerina cyanea*
    Lazuli: *Passerina amoena*
Cardinal, Northern: *Cardinalis cardinalis*
Chickadee
    Black-capped: *Parus atricapillus*
    Carolina: *Parus carolinensis*
Cowbird, Brown-headed: *Molothrus ater*
Creeper, Brown: *Certhia americana*
Cuckoo, Yellow-billed: *Coccyzus americanus*
Dove, Mourning: *Zenaida macroura*
Dove, Rock (see Rock Pigeon)
Duck, Wood: *Aix sponsa*
Falcon, Peregrine: *Falco peregrinus*
Finch
    House: *Carpodacus mexicanus*
    Purple: *Carpodacus purpureus*
Flycatcher
    Ash-throated: *Myiarchus cinerascens*
    Great Crested: *Myiarchus crinitus*
Goldfinch, American: *Carduelis tristis*
Goose, Canada: *Branta canadensis*
Harrier, Northern: *Circus cyaneus*
Hawk
    Broad-winged: *Buteo platypterus*
    Sharp-shinned: *Accipiter striatus*
Heron, Great Blue *Ardea herodias*
Hummingbird
    Anna's: *Calypte anna*
    Ruby-throated: *Archilochus colubris*
    Rufous: *Selasphorus rufus*

Jay
    Blue: *Cyanocitta cristata*
    Western Scrub: *Aphelocoma californica*
Junco, Dark-eyed: *Junco hyemalis*
Meadowlark
    Eastern: *Sturnella magna*
    Western: *Sturnella neglecta*
Nighthawk, Common: *Chordeiles minor*
Nuthatch, White-breasted: *Sitta carolinensis*
Owl
    Eastern Screech-: *Otus asio*
    Short-eared: *Asio flammeus*
    Snowy: *Nyctea scandiaca*
    Western Screech-: *Otus kennicottii*
Pigeon, Rock (formerly Rock Dove): *Columba livia*
Robin, American: *Turdus migratorius*
Sapsucker
    Red-breasted: *Sphyrapicus ruber*
    Williamson's: *Sphyrapicus thyroideus*
    Yellow-bellied: *Sphyrapicus varius*
Siskin, Pine: *Carduelis pinus*
Sparrow
    House: *Passer domesticus*
    White-throated: *Aonotrichia albicollis*
Starling, European: *Sturnus vulgaris*
Swallow
    Tree: *Tachycineta bicolor*
    Violet-green: *Tachycineta thalassina*
Thrush
    Hermit: *Catharus guttatus*
    Wood: *Hylocichla mustelina*
Titmouse, Tufted: *Parus bicolor*
Towhee
    Eastern: *Pipilo erythrophthal*
    Spotted: *Pipilo maculatus*
Turkey, Wild: *Meleagris gallopavo*
Vireo, Red-eyed: *Vireo olivaceus*
Waterthrush, Louisiana: *Seiurus motacilla*
Whip-poor-will: *Caprimulgus vociferus*
Woodpecker
    Downy: *Picoides pubescens*
    Golden-fronted: *Melanerpes aurifrons*

Hairy: *Picoides villosus*
Pileated: *Dyocopus pileatus*
Red-bellied: *Melanerpes carolinus*
Wren
Carolina: *Thryothorus ludovicianus*
House: *Troglodytes aedon*

Fish

Goldfish, Common (Chinese): *Carassius auratus*
Koi, Japanese: *Cyprinus carpio*

Insects

Ant: order Hymenoptera
Aphid: family *Aphididae*
Bee
American Bumble: *Bombus pennsylvanicus*
Carpenter
Eastern: *Xylocopa virginica*
Western: *Xylocopa californica*
Honey: *Apis mellifera*
Beetle
Carrion: family Silphidae
Chafer, Shining Leaf: subfamily Rutelinae
Japanese: *Popilla japonica*
Ladybug: family Coccinellidae
Lightning bug (or firefly): family Lampyridae
Rove, Gold-and-brown: *Ontholestes cingulatus*
Blowfly: genus *Protocalliphora*
Bug
Assassin: family Reduviidae
Milkweed
Large: *Oncopeltus fasciatus*
Small: *Lycaeus kalmii*
Butterfly: order Lepidoptera
Emperor, Hackberry: *Asterocampa celtis*
Monarch: *Danaus plexippus*
Red Admiral: *Vanessa atalanta*
Swallowtail, Anise: *Papilio zelicaon*
Swallowtail, Eastern Tiger: *Papilio glaucus*
Swallowtail, Spicebush: *Papilio troilus*
Swallowtail, Western: *Papilio rutulus*

Damselfly and Dragonfly: order Odonata
  Dragonfly, Common White-tailed: *Libellula lydia*
Diving Beetle, Predaceous: family Dytiscidae
Fly: order Diptera
  Bee: order Diptera
  Robber: family Asilidae
Hopper, Plant: family Fulgoridae
Hornet, European: family Vespidae
Mantid: family Mantidae
  Carolina: *Stagmomantis carolina*
  Chinese: *Tenodera aridifolia*
  European: *Mantis religiosa*
Mosquito: family Culicidae
Moth: order Lepidoptera
  Bagworm, Evergreen: *Thyridopteryx ephemeraeformis*
  Clearwing, Snowberry: *Hemaris diffinis*
  Clymene: *Haploa clymene*
  Sphinx
    Laurel: *Sphinx kalmiae*
    White-lined: *Hyles lineata*
Strider (also known as Skater), Common Water: *Gerris remigis*
Termite: order Isoptera
Tree Cricket, Snowy: *Oecanthus fultoni* Walker
Wasp: order Hymenoptera
  Spider: family Pompilidae
  Small Chalcid: *Nasonia vitripennis*

Invertebrates
Centipede: class Chilopoda
Earthworm: family Lumbricidae
Millipede: class Diplopoda
Pill or Sow Bugs: order Isopoda
Slug: many species in phylum Mollusca
Snail, Garden: family Helicidae

Mammals
Bat: order Chiroptera
  Evening: *Nycticeius humeralis*
Bear, American Black: *Ursus americanus*
Bison, American (or Buffalo): *Bos bison*

Cat, House: *Felis catus*
Cougar, Eastern (or Mountain Lion): *Felis concolor*
Coyote (or Brush Wolf, Prairie Wolf): *Canis latrans*
Deer
    Mule (sometimes called Black-tailed): *Odocoileus hemionus*
    White-tailed: *Odocoileus virginianus*
Dog (domestic): *Canis familiaris*
Elk: *Cervus elaphus*
Fox
    Gray: *Urocyon cinereoargenteus*
    Red: *Vulpes fulva*
Groundhog (or Woodchuck): *Marmota monax*
Human: *Homo sapiens*
Llama: *Lama* species
Mole
    Common (or Eastern): *Scalopus aquaticus*
    Star-nosed: *Condylura cristata*
    Townsend's: *Scapanus townsendi*
Mouse
    Deer: *Peromysais maniculatus*
    White-footed: *Peromyscus leucopus*
Opossum, Virginia: *Didelphis marsupialis*
Rabbit, Eastern Cottontail: *Sylvilagus floridanus*
Raccoon, Common: *Procyon lotor*
Shrew
    Least: *Cryptotis parva*
    Northern Short-tailed: *Blarina brevicauda*
Skunk
    Spotted: *Spilogale putorius*
    Striped: *Mephitis mephitis*
Squirrel, Tree
    Eastern Fox: *Sciurus niger*
    Eastern Gray: *Sciurus carolinensis*
    Flying, Northern: *Glaucomys sabrinus*
    Flying, Southern: *Glaucomys volans*
Vole, Meadow: *Microtus pennsylvanicus*
Wolf
    Brush (more commonly known as Coyote): *Canis latrans*
    Gray (or Timber): *Canis lupus*
Woodchuck (or Groundhog): *Marmota monax*

Reptiles

Lizard, Fence
  Eastern: *Sceloporus undulatus*
  Western: *Sceloporus occidentalis*
Snake: suborder Serpentes
  Black Rat: *Elaphe obsoleta*
  Water, Northern: *Nerodia sipedon*
  Worm: *Carphophis amoenus*
Turtle
  Eastern Box: *Terrapene carolina*
  Snapping: *Chelydra serpentina*

Plants

Flowers

Basil, Sweet Purple Ruffled: *Ocimum basilicum*
Bee Balm (or Oswego Tea): *Monarda didyma*
Bitter Cress, Small-flowered: *Cardamine parviflora*
Black-eyed Susan: *Rudbeckia hirta*
Clover, White: *Trifolium repens*
Daffodil: *Narcissus* species
Daisy, Shasta: *Chysanthemum x superbum*
Dandelion, Common: *Taraxacum officinale*
Daylily: *Hemerocallis fulva*
Dutchman's Breeches: *Dicentra cucullaria*
Four-o'clock: *Mirabilis jalapa*
Fuchsia, Honeysuckle: *Fuchsia triphylla* 'Thalia'
Impatiens: *Impatiens* species
  Jewelweed: *Impatiens capensis*
Ironweed, New York: *Vernonia noveboracensis*
Jack-in-the-pulpit: *Arisaema atrorubens*
Lily, Asiatic and Oriental: *Lillium* species
Milkweed, Common: *Asclepias syriaca*
Obedient Plant: *Physostegia* species
Perennial Pea: *Lathyrus latifolius*
Plantain, Common: *Plantago major*
Sedum: *Sedum* species
Speedwell, Persian: *Veronica persica*
Spring Beauty: *Claytonia virginica*
Sunflower: *Helianthus annuus*

Venus's Looking-glass: *Specularia perfoliata*
Violet: *Viola* species
Wild Bergamot: *Monarda fistulosa*
Yarrow: *Achillea millifolium*

Grasses
Lawn, Northern
    Fescue: *Festuca rubra*
    Kentucky Bluegrass: *Poa pretense*
Lawn, Southern
    Bermuda: *Cyodon dactylon*
    Zoysia: *Zoysia matrella*

Shrubs
Abelia: *Abelia* species
Azalea: *Rhodendron* species
Butterfly Bush: *Buddleia* species
Elderberry (or American Elder): *Sambucus canadensis*
Holly: *Ilex* species
    Japanese Hellerei: *Ilex crenata 'Hellerei'*
Mountain Laurel: *Kalmia latifolia*
Photinia, Chinese: *Photinia serrulata*
Rose, Meideland (Hardy Shrub): *Rosa* species
Shrub Althea (or Rose of Sharon): *Hibiscus syriacus*
Viburnum: *Viburnum* species
Weigela: *Weigela florida*
Winged Euonymus: *Euonymus alata*

Trees
Cedar, Eastern Red: *Juniperus virginiana*
Dogwood, Flowering: *Cornus florida*
Fringe Tree, Virginia: *Chionanthus virginicus*
Hackberry, Common: *Celtis occidentalis*
Maple, Japanese: *Acer palmatum*
Pawpaw: *Asimina triloba*
Pine: *Pinus* species
Sourwood: *Oxydendron arboreum*

Vines
Clematis: *Clematis* species
Ivy, English: *Hedera helix*

Morning Glory: *Ipomoea* species
Trumpet Creeper: *Campsis radicans*

Water Plants

Anacharis: *Elodea canadensis*
Cattail: *Typha* species
Flag, Sweet: *Acorus calamus*
Hardy Perennial Water Lily: *Nymphaea* species
Hardy Thalia: *Thalia dealbata*

Birdseed Plants

Buckwheat: *Fagopyrum sagittatum*
Canary: *Phalaris canariensis*
Corn: *Zea mays*
Milo: *Sorghum vulgare*
Oats: *Avena sativa*
Peanuts: *Arachis hypogaea*
Proso Millet—Red or White: *Panicum miliaceum*
Safflower: *Carthamus tincorius*
Sunflower: *Helianthus annuus*
Thistle (or Niger, Nyjer): *Guizotia abyssinica*
Wheat: *Triticum aestivum*

Resources

Local knowledgeable people are often your best guides to what plants will do well and what kinds of wildlife live in your area. This section provides general categories of institutions, organizations, governmental agencies, stores, and catalogs that can be sources of specific advice. You can also use the Internet, contact the reference desk of your local public library, and check listings in the local phone book. Read local newspapers and other publications for announcements of meetings and talks that are open to the public.

Universities and Colleges

Some colleges, especially community colleges, offer noncredit courses in nature and gardening subjects. These are especially beneficial if you find it easier to learn in a more formal and structured environment. But the real advantage of taking such courses is the opportunity to get to know other people who share your interests. You can discuss your experiences and ask questions of one another, all of which will increase your knowledge. And your interactions can continue long after the class has ended.

Institutions of higher learning that offer horticulture, natural resources, forestry, or wildlife management courses may have professors who are willing to answer a few questions. Keep in mind, however, that these folks have a job to do, so you should not monopolize their time. Find out if there is an extension professor whose responsibilities include answering questions from the public.

Check under county agencies in the phone book to see if there is an extension office near you. Extension programs allow universities to extend their educational reach geographically. The main job of county extension agents is to give assistance to the public.

Organizations

In most areas, you can find local gardening and birding clubs or societies. Some areas may have reptile and amphibian or butterfly clubs. You can usually attend a meeting for free to check out the club and then perhaps pay a small fee to join it if you enjoyed the experience. Your club dues might entitle you to newsletters, a discount on birdseed, the opportunity to buy locally grown plants (if the club holds sales to raise money), trip opportunities, and meetings with knowledgeable speakers. Joining a club may be even more helpful than taking a class because of the variety of activities you can take advantage of. And because clubs tend to meet regularly throughout the year, it is easier to keep up with breaking news (such as what birds have arrived for the winter or if particular plants are blooming earlier than usual).

There are often state and national clubs as well. These larger organizations usually have more comprehensive newsletters or full-fledged magazines. Their meetings may be less frequent than those of local clubs, and they are usually held in different locations so that all members have a chance to attend at least once a year without traveling a great distance. Annual trips may be organized to view wildlife or plants.

Following is a list of some national organizations that you might like to join. Many of these groups also have chapters at the state level.

American Birding Association
Ducks Unlimited
Izaak Walton League of America
National Arbor Day Foundation
National Audubon Society
National Institute for Urban Wildlife
National Wildlife Federation
The Nature Conservancy
North American Butterfly Association
Sierra Club
Trout Unlimited

Governmental Agencies

Numerous state and federal government agencies exist whose partial mission is to provide information to the public. If contacting one agency does not result in an answer to your question, ask for a recommendation regarding where you might try next. Eventually you should get to the right agency.

At some point, you may wish to contact one or more of the following federal agencies. The main focus of each is evident from its name.

National Park Service
U.S. Department of Agriculture
U.S. Environmental Protection Agency
U.S. Fish and Wildlife Service
U.S. Forest Service

State governments usually maintain a variety of offices that deal with the environment. The names of state agencies fulfilling the functions in the generalized categories listed below vary from state to state. Check the local phone book or contact your local public library to determine the exact title of the agency in your state that deals with the subject of interest.

Conservation
Environmental regulation
Extension
Forestry
Freshwater and marine resources
Game and wildlife
Soil and water

Commercial Sources

Plant nurseries and specialty stores (such as nature stores or those that specialize in items for birds) are usually staffed by people with a keen interest in the products offered for sale. These salespeople can give you fairly reliable advice about what plants will perform well where you live and what products might be best for your situation. However, keep in mind that even with informed suggestions, you will invariably suffer some disappointments. For whatever reason—local site conditions, inexperience, a determined critter—sometimes you will not achieve good results.

As a general rule, nursery staff can tell you whether a plant is hardy and suitable for your area, but they may not be able to tell you whether it is useful to wildlife. College horticulture departments do not normally train their students about the needs of wildlife. Therefore, you have to do your homework before you head to the nursery.

Sometimes you can find a larger selection of plants in gardening catalogs. If you buy plants or seeds from a catalog, however, buy from a supplier whose climatic conditions are similar to those where you live. Plants acclimatized to colder or warmer conditions may not fare well in your locale.

Plant experts always advise you to buy only from reputable nurseries, not from discount, grocery, or department stores, where the staff may not be knowledgeable about plants and therefore may not have cared for them properly. The potted plants may be over- or underwatered, unfertilized, or subjected to temperature variations. Although these points are well taken, if you do not have a lot of money or nurseries are not conveniently located near your home, take heart. As long as a plant looks healthy and the soil shows no moss growth (which indicates that the plant has been continuously overwatered and may have root rot), the plant should survive and do as well as a more expensive, pampered plant from a nursery. Plants have evolved to withstand some adversity. After all, if they could not survive an occasional dry or wet spell or an overly warm or cold stretch, they would be doomed.

Similar advice applies to buying gardening and wildlife supplies. You will probably find that specialty stores and catalogs have the best selection of wildlife boxes, food, and gardening tools. But do not overlook your local discount and hardware stores, because they may sell some of the same items at a lower price or other good-quality items that are not available elsewhere. It is also useful to cultivate a relationship with staff of a nearby hardware store so that you can get their expert advice about such things as how to securely hang your birdhouses and feeders.

Never be embarrassed to seek information. The saying "knowledge is power" is right on the money—and it could save *you* money in the long run.